The New York Agent Book

Get the Agent you need for the career you want

K CALLAN

✦ Fifth Edition
revised and updated

© 1987, 1990, 1993, 1995, 1998 K Callan
ISBN 1-878355-07-4
ISSN 1058-1928

Other books by K Callan
An Actor's Workbook
Directing your directing career
How to sell yourself as an actor
The Los Angeles Agent Book
The Life of the Party
The Script is finished, Now what do I do?

Illustrations: Barry Wetmore
Map: Kelly Callan
Photography: ABC Television
Editor: Kristi Nolte

✦ Introduction

Directors, producers, agents and civilians (people not in the business) frequently comment to me that my books about the entertainment industry follow a circuitous route. Actors never say that. They know the business *is* a circuitous route. You enter the circle anyplace and usually don't get to choose where. It is possible to spend 20 years at this occupation and still feel like a beginner, depending on what phase of the career you are experiencing.

The periods of heat in a career make an actor think he will never be unemployed again (no matter what he has witnessed or experienced before) and the periods of unemployment produce only a different agitated state: *I'll never work again. It was all an accident. Now, they know I can't act. I just fooled them before.*

Some young actors waltz in, get attention, an agent and a job, and aren't seriously unemployed for 10 or 20 years. When things inevitably slow down, they have to learn the business skills that other less fortunate actors began to learn on day one. There are no steps to be skipped as it turns out. We all just take them at different times.

As important as business skills is self-knowledge. Although some actors never have to find a niche for themselves, most of us spend several years figuring out just what it is we have to sell. If you weigh 500 pounds, it doesn't take a master's degree to figure out that you're going to play the fat one. If you go on a diet and become a more average size, casting directors will have a harder time pegging which one you are and you may, too. This is not to say that if you are easily typed that your life is bed of roses, but it can be a lot easier.

So, *Self-Knowledge* could be Chapter One for one actor and the end of the book for someone else. An actor who already has an agent might feel justified in starting with Chapter Ten because he wants to change agents while a newcomer in town might feel that divorce is not the problem he's currently confronted with. At this point, all he wants is an agent — any agent.

In fact, a beginning actor would gain insight from Chapter Ten. That information could alert him to potential warning signs when he *is* meeting with an agent and Chapter One might prompt the seasoned actor to re-examine all the things his agent does do for him.

This book deals with all aspects of actor/agent relationships at various stages of one's career: the first agent, the freelance alliance, the exclusive relationship, confronting the agent with problems, salvaging the bond, and if need be, leaving the partnership.

There is information for the newcomer, help for the seasoned actor and encouragement for everybody.

My consciousness about the business has been dramatically raised as a result of meeting and interviewing over 300 agents in New York and Los Angeles. The process was just like every other part of the business, sometimes scary, sometimes wonderful and sometimes painful, but always a challenge.

Mostly, the agents were funny, interesting, dynamic, warm and not at all as unapproachable as they seem when you are outside the office looking in.

Regardless of the circular nature of the business and this book, my strong advice to you is to read *straight through* and not skip around. The first part provides background to critically understanding the information in the latter part of the book.

Fight the urge to run to the agency listings and read about this agent or that. Until you digest more criteria regarding evaluating agents you may find yourself just as confused as before.

If you read the agents' quotes with some perception, you will gain insights not only into their character but into how the business really runs. You will notice whose philosophy coincides with yours. Taken by themselves the quotes might only be interesting but considered in context and played against the insights of other agents, they are revealing and educational.

I have quoted a few agents that you will not find

listed here because they are either from Los Angeles (Ken Kaplan, Tim Angle), out of the business (Joanna Ross, Lynn Moore Oliver, Meg Mortimer) or deceased (Michael Kingman, Barry Douglas). Even though you won't be able to consider them as possible business partners, I felt their insights were particularly valuable.

Check all addresses before mailing. Every effort has been made to provide accurate and current addresses and phone numbers, but agents move and computers goof. Call the office and verify the address. They won't know it's you.

It's been a gratifying experience to come in contact with all the agents and all the actors I have met as a result of my books. Because I am asking the questions for all of us, if I've missed something you deem important, tell me and I'll include it in my next book. Write to me c/o Sweden Press at the address on the back of the book or at my e-mail address: SwedenPr@aol.com.

K Callan
Los Angeles, California

✦ Table of Contents

1 Avenues of Opportunity

Many actors regularly curse and malign agents. They either feel rejected that they can't get an agent to talk to them or frustrated once they have an agent because sometimes actors have unrealistic expectations. You can save yourself a lot of heartache by learning how the business really works and how agents do their jobs.

What *is* an agent anyway? What does an agent do? Where do I find one? Do I need one? How can I get one to talk to me? What would I say to an agent? Are there rules of behavior? How can I tell if someone is a good agent? When is the right time to look for one? If they all want to sign me, how can I choose the right one? If no one wants to sign me, what will I tell my mother?

Let's dispense with the mother issue right off. Unless your mother is an actress, she is never going to understand. Those (civilians and would-be actors who are still in school) who have never pursued a job in show business can never understand what an actor goes through in pursuit of employment and/or an agent, so don't waste time on that conversation. Just say: *Mom, I'm doing great. I'm unemployed right now and I don't have an agent, but that's part of the process. There are things I need to accomplish before it's time for me to look for an agent.*

She can repeat that to her friends. She's not going to understand, but it will mean something to her that you have a plan.

What Is An Agent?

Whether your agent fantasy includes the old-fashioned stereotype of cigar-chomping hustlers or the newer version of the cool customer in the expensive Armani suit, many actors fantasize that the right agent holds the secret of success. Joanna Ross was an agent at

William Morris before she left the business and moved to Italy, but I'm still quoting her because her perspective on the actor/agent relationship is so insightful.

◆ *Actors feel that if they make the right choice that somehow the agent is going to make them a star and help them be successful, or they're going to make the wrong choice and that's it. And that's just not it.*

No agent can make anybody a star or make them a better actor than they are. Agents are only avenues of opportunity.

Joanna Ross

That being the case, what do these Avenues of Opportunity do? The dictionary (which knows very little about show business) has several definitions for the word *agent*. By combining a couple, I've come up with: *A force acting in place of another, effecting a certain result by driving, inciting, or setting in motion.*

So?

In its simplest incarnation, the agent, acting on your behalf, sets in motion a series of events that result in your having a shot at a job. He gets you meetings, interviews and auditions. And he prays that you will get the job or at the very least make him look good by being brilliant.

When an actor is grousing that the agent is not getting him out, he seems to think the agent doesn't want him to work — completely forgetting that if the actor doesn't work, the agent cannot pay his rent. Not only that, the actor overlooks the fact that his part of the partnership is to get the job.

It should be simple to get the job, really. After all, you have spent years studying, perfecting your instrument, training your body, voice, craft and personality, and building a resume that denotes credibility. Haven't you?

While you have been working on every aspect of your craft, the agent you want has spent his time getting to know the business. He's seen every play, television show and film. He's watched actors, writers, directors and producers birth their careers and grow. He's tracked people on every level of the business. He has networked, stayed visible and communicated. He's made it his business to meet and develop relationships with casting directors.

The agent you want only represents those actors whose work he personally knows so that when he tells a casting director that an actor is perfect for the role and has the background for it, the casting director trusts his word. That's the way the agent builds *his* credibility. It doesn't happen any faster than the building of the actor's resume.

In addition to getting the actor the appropriate audition, the agent has to be prepared to negotiate a brilliant contract when the actor wins the job. That entails knowing all the contracts, rules and regulations of the Screen Actors Guild, Actors Equity, and American Federation of Television and Radio Artists, as well as having an understanding of the marketplace and knowing what others at similar career levels are getting for similar jobs.

He must then have the courage, style and judgment to stand up to the buyers in asking what is fair for the actor without becoming too grandiose and turning everyone off. And the agent must fight the temptation to sell the actor down the river financially in order to seal the agent's future relationships with the producers or casting directors.

What Do Agents Think Their Job Is?

✦ *I feel that I'm responsible for my clients' attitudes and for*

their self-confidence.
Kenneth Kaplan
The Gersh Agency, Inc.

Ambrosio/Mortimer has closed and Meg Mortimer is presently on hiatus from the business, but she has such insightful thoughts that I am including them.

✦   *The agent needs to be open and imaginative about the kinds of roles the actor can play, given the actor's range, where he is in his career, and what would be a terrific career move.*

The agent needs to give his personal advice based on his experience as to the actor's next career choice. Sometimes the actor just needs to make a living, but mostly it's about how can he have a successful and well-rounded career.

Maybe the actor needs to move to the West Coast or maybe he needs to take an out of town tour in order to bring the career to a different level. Sometimes it's important to take the low budget film instead of the TV series.

It's the agent's job to be the buffer zone. He needs to be the bad cop at the negotiation, fighting for the best deal, but protecting the actor from that battle. Negotiation is a big part of the agent's job.
Meg Mortimer

✦   *I have tried, with as much speed as possible, to let clients know that this is really an alliance that's built and that it's very much a commitment. I want them to know that eventually they can truly feel comfortable not seeking the approval of their agents. The confidence factor is so important to an actor. He is at the mercy of so many people.*

If the actor can sense a comfortability and a compatibility with his agent, then communication comes, along with real trust. Then you really work in tandem with each other. It becomes a mutuality.
Peter Strain
Peter Strain & Associates

✦   *If you sign someone, if you agree to be their agent, no matter how big the agency gets, you've agreed to be there for them and that's your responsibility.*

Kenneth Kaplan
The Gersh Agency, Inc.

✦   *I offer hard work and honesty and demand the same in return. If I'm breaking my ass to get you an audition, you better show up.*

Martin Gage
The Gage Group

Although it might be nice to be pals with your agent, it is not necessary. One of the best agents I ever had was never available to help me feel good when all was dark.

He did, however, initiate new business for me, was respected in the community, negotiated well, had impeccable taste and access to everyone in the business. He also believed in me and did not lose faith when I did not win every audition. He gave me good notes on my performances, clued me as to mistakes I was making, and made a point of viewing my work at every opportunity. Oh yes, *and* he returned my phone calls!

A friend of mine who toiled for many years on a well-regarded series, was happy to be working, but felt her agent had not negotiated well. She changed agents and doubled her salary. A year later, she changed agents again: *They were good negotiators, but I couldn't stand talking to them.*

You can't have everything.

Being a tough negotiator sometimes displaces graciousness. So maybe your agent won't be your best friend. He's not supposed to be, he's your business partner. You have to decide what you want and what you need.

Ex-Los Angeles agent, Lynn Moore Oliver gives us a much clearer picture of what agents are doing in our behalf, even when we can't tell they are even thinking about us:

+ *I'm working on the belief that symbiotically we're going to build a career. While the actor isn't working, I'm paying for the phone, the stationery, the envelopes, the Breakdown Service (which is expensive), the messenger service to send the pictures around, the rent, the overhead, stamps, all the things that one takes for granted in the normal turn of business. All this is coming out of my pocket working as an employment agent, because that is really what I am.*

The actor is making no investment in my promoting his career. If the career is promoted, we both benefit and I take my 10% commission. Meanwhile the overhead goes on for months, sometimes years with no income. The first thing the actor is going to say is, Nothing's happening. My agent is not doing a good job. *What they forget is that I have actually invested money in their career and probably I've invested more money in the actor's career than he has, on an annual basis.*

If you think about what Lynn says, you will understand why credible agents choose clients carefully. Looking at your actor friends, are there any that you would be willing to put on *your* list and pay to promote? Puts things more in perspective, doesn't it?

Franchised Agents

An actor who is a member of one of the performers' unions must be represented by a franchised agent. The actor can represent himself anytime he wants, but if an agent conducts business for him, the agent must have signed an agreement with one of the performers' unions. That agreement is called a franchise.

To be a franchised agent, the agent must have a license to operate from the state, agree to abide by the Agency Rules and Regulations of the union, have some experience as an agent and put up a financial bond. None of this guarantees the agent to be ethical, knowledgeable or effective. You'll have to check that yourself.

Sexual Harassment

If someone is going to either represent you or give you a part in return for sexual favors (doubtful, at best), I don't think that's a part that is going to build your career.

If you suspect that an agent has bad intentions, if he makes moves on you in even the most subtle way, back off. This is not what the agent of your dreams is going to do. If you call the union to confirm your suspicions, the union is legally not allowed to give you any information unless charges have been filed, an investigation has been conducted and a judge has made some ruling. Anything else is just hearsay and the union can be sued for damages for passing that information along. The union will be very helpful if you have a problem and intend to file charges, but you have to be prepared to go on record.

It's up to you to be smart, do research, stay alert and notice what is going on. You can smell when things are weird. It may be titillating and make you feel chosen momentarily if an agent comes on to you, but in the long run, it will cost you. You will always be vulnerable to that person and who's to say he/she will keep his end of the bargain?

This kind of behavior is more interesting to view in a movie than in real life. Don't put yourself in compromising situations.

Stay focused on business. Educate yourself so that you can make an intelligent decision about which agents to pursue and choose.

Wrap Up

Agent

✓ a force acting in place of another, effecting a certain result by driving, inciting, or setting in motion
✓ an avenue of opportunity
✓ regulated by the unions — up to a point

Agent's Job

✓ to get the actor meetings, interviews, auditions and to negotiate salary and billing

Sexual Harassment

✓ be alert
✓ you don't have to put up with it
✓ don't play into it

2   Your First Agent

There's good news and bad news. First the bad news: you're probably going to have to be your own first agent. Now, the good news: nobody cares more about your career than you do, so your first agent is going to be incredibly motivated.

In order to attract an agent, you have to have something to sell. No matter how talented you are, if you don't have some way to show what you've got, you're all talk. Working up a scene for the agent's office will work for a few agents, but basically, it's not enough. Your focus at this point has to be to amass credits by appearing onstage so an agent can see your work, or working in student and independent films, so you can put together a professional audition tape.

The New York Agent Book is focused on people who are already entrepreneurial. For those of you who need help in that department, get my marketing book, *How to Sell Yourself as an Actor*. It will help you focus.

✦   *Unless you're 17 and gorgeous, it's a waste of time to make rounds. Ringing doorbells, slipping pictures under doors, sending pictures. We probably get about 15 pictures a day — that's how we get our cardboard.*

Unless Meg Simon or someone recommends you, it's pretty impossible. I think they should knock themselves out trying to get a valid showcase. Lord knows that's hard, but it can't be any harder than ringing doorbells trying to get a good agent..
Monty Silver
Silver, Massetti & Szatmary, East Ltd.

I know what you are thinking: *Swell. How am I going to amass credits and put together a professional tape without an agent? How am I ever going to get any work?*

By just doing it. Start taking action. Pick up *Backstage* or *ShowBusiness* for casting notices. Get onto the actor's grapevine by joining a theatre group or getting into an acting class.

✦   *I would go to class. I would do anything I could. I would not sit around feeling sorry for myself. If I couldn't get someone to hire me as an actor, I'd get a group of my friends in the same position; I'd move all the furniture to one side and I'd do a play in my living room and then call the agents and ask them to come see me.*

Lionel Larner
Lionel Larner, Ltd.

That's exactly what Carol Burnett did when she first came to New York. Her autobiography, *One More Time* (Random House, 1986) is filled with inspiration.

Preparation

In order to agent yourself, you will need to do all the things we talked about agents doing in Chapter One. Check the paragraph entitled *An Agent Prepares* on page 3. You're not going to just waltz in and meet agents and casting executives, but as you begin to make friends with others in the business who are on your level, you will be surprised how one thing leads to another.

✦   *If I were an actor just in from the boondocks without any experience whatsoever, I think I would get myself hired somewhere in a theatre; I mean doing anything, selling programs or candy or watching the phone, or the stage door. I would get myself a job in the business because you learn a tremendous amount. I also think it shows the determination because you're not looking immediately for the reward before doing the work. We all have to pay our dues.*

Lionel Larner
Lionel Larner, Ltd.

Becoming an actor is not an overnight process. A large part of being an actor on any level is looking for work. Don't equate being paid with being an actor. You are already an actor. Even if you are a student actor, you're still an actor and you actually have your first assignment: get a resume with decent credits and build an audition tape.

What denotes decent credits? Although agents are happy to see school and home town credits on a resume so they know you didn't just start yesterday, those credits not only don't mean much in the marketplaces of Los Angeles/New York/Chicago, they don't constitute an arena for the agent to see you in action first hand.

If, on the other hand, you are appearing in a decent venue where he can drop by and look at you or — if he is canvassing the town on his own — discover you, then you have the possibility of becoming a marketable commodity.

When you can also deliver an example of your work on videotape (an audition tape), you are in business.

The audition tape is a videotape usually no longer than eight minutes that shows either one performance or a montage of scenes of an actor's work. It is better to have just one good scene than many short moments of work. It's also not helpful to show several scenes from the same performance. Agents and casting executives view tapes endlessly so make yours short and effective. Always better to leave your audience wanting more.

Agents and casting directors prefer to see tapes featuring your appearances on television or film, though some will look at a tape produced solely for audition purposes. If you can't produce footage that shows you clearly in contemporary material playing a part that you could logically be cast for, then you aren't far enough along to make a tape yet. Better to wait than to show yourself at less than your best. Patience.

Pictures

There are many good photographers in town who make a business taking actors' headshots. They vary in price and product. I've gathered a list of favorites from agents, actors and casting directors.

Don't just choose one off the list. You need to do your own research on something as personal as a photograph. Make an appointment with at least three photographers to evaluate their book and how comfortable you feel with them. No matter how good his/her pictures are, if you don't feel at ease with that person, your pictures are going to reflect that, so take the time to evaluate your compatibility.

Look through *The Players Guide* and begin to notice what makes you look at one picture more than another. Look at the pictures your friends are using and find out about their photographers.

An expensive price tag doesn't guarantee a better picture. It's possible to get the perfect picture for under $200 and a picture you will never use at $650. Some photographers include hair and make-up artists as part of the price. That's nice, but make sure you are able to duplicate the look when you go on auditions. The number one dictate from casting directors about pictures is *what you see is what you get*. Casting directors don't like surprises. If your picture looks like Kim Basinger and you look like Jennifer Jason Leigh, the casting director is not going to be happy when he calls you in to read. And vice versa.

Your picture and your reel are your main selling tools. Give them the care and attention they deserve.

The picture can be printed with or without a white border. Some agents prefer the picture without border, but it is usually more expensive. You can have your name printed on the front or not, either superimposed over the photo or in the white space below.

Casting directors just care that the picture look like you.

Photographers

Barbara Bordnick
Suzanne Gold
Lorin Klaris
Blanche Mackay

David Morgan
Tess Steinkolk
Van Williams (natural light)

Resume

A resume is sent along with your 8x10 glossy or matte print. Your resume should be stapled to the back so that as you turn the picture over, you see the resume as though it were printed on the back side of the photo. The buyers see hundreds of resumes every day, so make yours simple and easy to read. It's not necessary to have millions of jobs listed. When prospective employers see too much writing, their eyes glaze over and they won't read anything so be brief.

Choose the most impressive credits and list them. There is an example on page 14 to use as a guide for form. Lead with your strong suit. If you have done more commercials than anything else, list that as your first category; if you are a singer, list music. You may live in a market where theatre credits are taken very seriously. If this is so, even though you may have done more commercials, lead with theatre if you have anything credible to report.

Adapt this example to meet your needs. If all you have done is college theatre, list that. This is more than someone else has done and it will give the buyer an idea of parts you can play. Note that you were master of ceremonies for your town Pioneer Day Celebration. If you sing, list where. Accomplishments that might seem trivial to you could be important to someone else, particularly if you phrase it right. As you acquire more important credits, drop the less important ones.

Mary Smith/212-555-4489
5'4", 115 lbs, blonde hair, blue eyes

Theatre

Hamlet .... theatre or director
Lost in Yonkers .... theatre or director

Film

Perfect Murder .... Andrew Davis
In &Out .... Frank Oz

Television

Spin City .... director
Law and Order .... director

Training

Acting .... teacher
Singing .... teacher
Dance .... teacher

Special Skills

play guitar, horseback riding, martial arts, Spanish
dialect, etc.

My advice is not to list union affiliation
(Screen Actors Guild, Actors Equity Association,
American Federation of Television and Radio Artists)
on the resume. As far I am concerned, if you list them,
you are making a big deal of it. If you are a member of
the unions, let that be taken as a matter of course. If
you are not that far along yet, don't bring it to their
attention.

I also doubt that it's helpful to list extra work on a resume. While work as an extra gives you the opportunity to be on the set to see what things are like, I don't think it enhances a resume for an actor who wants to do more than extra work.

If you are truly beginning and have nothing for your resume, at least list your training and a physical description along with the names of your teachers.

The most important thing on your resume is your name and your agent's phone number. If you don't have an agent, get phone mail for work calls, don't use your personal phone number. It's not only safer, but more professional.

Open Calls

Although Equity Open Calls are limited to members of Actors Equity, in 1988 the National Labor Relations Board required that producers hold open calls for non-union actors. These auditions can be harrowing with hundreds of actors signing up for a small number of jobs, but people do get jobs there.

✦   *Actors Equity surveyed 500 members and found that 47% had found jobs through open casting calls. In calls for chorus work, which has its own system, casting directors size up the hopefuls who show up and point to those who resemble the type they are seeking before holding auditions.*
The Early Bird Gets the Audition
Jennifer Kingson Bloom
The New York Times
March 23, 1995

It's not just wearing for the actors; the producers, directors and casting executives also find it daunting.

✦ *Only 100 were given a chance to sing half a song and hoof a few steps. Vincent G. Liff, the casting director for* Big *and* Phantom of the Opera, *who turned away no less than 250 women for* Big *alone, called the turnout* frightening *but said the system, while patience-trying, was valuable.* We have cast dozens and dozens of people through these calls, Mr. Liff *said.*

The Early Bird Gets the Audition
Jennifer Kingson Bloom
The New York Times
March 23, 1995

Stand-Up Performers

A videotape is also a good selling tool for stand-up performers. Better, though, is time in front of an audience.

✦ *I would say to really know whether you have any place in the comedy business at all, that you would have to give yourself at least two years. Less than that is not enough. The first year you'll spend just trying to get your name around, trying to get people to know who you are so they will give you some stage time. It's a long trip. Just like an actor.*

Don't seek representation with five minutes of material. You need to keep working. The next thing to do is to try to get work in road clubs. It's very important to get the experience. There is limited experience if you just stay in one city.
Bruce Smith
Omnipop

The most successful people in any business are smart, organized and entrepreneurial. As you continue reading agents' remarks about what successful actors do, you will begin to develop an overview of the business that will help you in the process of representing yourself. Stay focused and specific.

Bring the same creative problem-solving you

use in preparing a scene to the business side of your career. You will not only be successful, you will begin to feel more in control of your own destiny.

Wrap Up

Tools for First Agent

✓ decent credits
✓ open calls
✓ audition tape

3 Welcome to the Big Apple

If you've just come to the New York City, no matter how long you have waited to get here, you will need a period of adjustment. Don't add the stress of agent-hunting until you have an apartment and are ready to be seen.

Get A Place To Live

Even though it's New York, the problem is not unsolvable. If you are a union member, check out the union bulletin boards for sublet information. The bulletin boards at The Drama Book Shop and wherever you might be taking classes are also good sources for information on temporary housing. The show business newspapers *Backstage* and *ShowBusiness* also offer opportunities to plug into the grapevine.

There are actor-friendly neighborhoods in the City: West Beth (downtown in the West Village) and The Manhattan Plaza (midtown on the West Side) are both artistic communities with subsidized housing and long waiting lists, but sublets are available since actors are frequently out of town for jobs. Both of these artists' havens offer classes and are plugged into the creative forces of the city.

Areas in which rents are cheaper are the Lower East Side, below Wall Street, Chinatown, and some areas of what used to be called Hell's Kitchen in the far West 40s.

Some churches and YMCA/YWCAs have a limited amount of relatively inexpensive housing available on a temporary basis. There is also a Youth Hostel in New York. For information consult The New York Convention and Visitors Bureau, Two Columbus Circle, New York, NY 10019.

There are those fabled $75 per month apartments that keep us all salivating but they have been occupied for hundreds of years by the same tenant. Don't allow yourself to keep from finding suitable housing because you are waiting for one of those fabulous deals. You don't want to use up all your good luck getting a swell apartment for 35¢. Save your luck for your big break and you'll be able to afford to pay full price.

More and more people are finding housing in Brooklyn, Queens, New Jersey and Staten Island. When I first arrived in New York, I briefly considered New Jersey (since I had children), but after much soul-searching, I realized that my dream was to come to New York City. I decided that if I was going to starve, it would be while living my dream all the way. Not everyone's dream is so particularized. There are many actors who live out of the city successfully and prefer it.

✦ *Get a job. Keep yourself in a good state all of the time. You can't be broke. It does not work. Secure yourself a job in whatever it is that you can do, whether it be as a waiter or as a secretary, where they give you leniency to go out on auditions. Being a starving actor does not work. What works is to be healthy and to keep some money in your pocket so that you are not hysterical while you are doing this. I don't come from the point of view that you have to suffer to be an actor.*
Bruce Levy
Bruce Levy Agency

✦ *Before an actor begins to look for an agent, he should establish a secure foundation. He or she needs a place to live and/or a job and some friends to talk to and pictures or at least a facsimile of pictures. It's very important that they have a comfortable place to go to during the day and be settled so they don't carry any more anxiety than necessary into an agent or manager's office.*

Actors think an agent or a manager will turn into a surrogate mother-father-teacher-confessor and that really isn't their role. Actors get disappointed when they aren't taken care of right away. I think it's better to come in as a fully secure person so you can be sold that way. Otherwise, too much development time is wasted.

Gary Krasny
The Krasny Office

First impressions are always the strongest, make sure yours is a good one. As J. Michael Bloom puts it: *You're only new once.*

✦ *You want to come to New York with training and with a base because when you meet people, the way you are at that moment is how they're going to remember you. If you meet people and you're not at your best, that's going to be the way they remember you.*

It's all those silly things your mother told you when you were growing up. You hated it, but she was right all along. Teachers do always remember you as you are the first day of class. Sometimes you can shift that image, but it's hard.

Flo Rothacker
DGRW

✦ *When I teach workshops, I notice that many young actors only want to get the agent and get the job and have an instant career. They want instant success before developing themselves and their craft. I tell all young actors: get in therapy, get into NYU, Yale, Juilliard, one of the league schools. Everyone at the leagues this year was doing scenes from movies. It seems that they all were interested in being celebrities.*

Jim Flynn
Berman, Boals and Flynn, Inc.

✦ *I think the philosophical basis is to work as much as possible, because the more you work, the more people have an opportunity to respond to it. Everyone in this business who is not an actor makes his living by recognizing talented actors.*

The smartest thing a young playwright can do is to get to know a good, young, talented actor so that when there is a showcase of the playwright's play, he can recommend the actor. That's going to make his play look better.

There are a number of stage directors in New York who, all they can really do (to be candid), is read a script and cast well and then stay out of the way. That can often be all you need.

Casting directors, agents, playwrights, directors, even stage managers are going to remember good actors. If they want to get ahead in their business, the more they remember good actors, the better off they're gonna be. Having your work out there is the crucial thing.

Studying is important because it keeps you ready. Nobody is going to give you six weeks to get your instrument ready. It's here's the audition; do it now, *so I believe in showcases. Actors tend to be too linear in their thinking. They think,* Okay. I did this showcase and no agent came and nobody asked me to come to their office so it was a complete waste of time.

Well, I don't believe that. First of all, even a bad production is going to teach a young actor a lot of important things. Second of all, generally, if you do a good job in a play, it produces another job. Often it's in another showcase. Often, it's a year later, so if you're looking for direct links, you never see them.

What tends to happen is somebody calls you up and says, I saw you in that show and you were really terrific and would you like to come do this show? *It's like out of the blue, and it can take a long time. You may have to do eight great showcases or readings, but if your work is out there, there is an opportunity for people to get excited and if it isn't out there, then that opportunity doesn't exist. It doesn't matter how terrific you are in the office and how charming you are. None of that matters.*

Tim Angle
Don Buchwald & Associates

Show business takes even balanced people and chews them up and spits them out for breakfast. Unless you are able to remain extremely focused and provide a personal life for yourself, you will have a difficult time dealing with the downs *and* ups of life as an actor, so either get into therapy or start meditating. Do whatever it takes to put your life in a heathy state.

✦   *There are some people I know who are brilliant actors, but I'm not willing to take responsibility for their careers because I know the rest of their life is not in order.*

Flo Rothacker
DGRW

If you are in an impossible relationship or if you have any kind of addiction problem, the business is only going to intensify it. Deal with these things first. If your life *is* in order, find a support group to help you keep it that way before you enter the fray.

People Who Need People

Life is easier with friends. Begin to build relationships with your peers. There are those who say you should build friendships with people who already have what you want. I understand that thinking, but it's not my idea of a good time.

It's a lot easier to live on a shoestring and/or deal with constant rejection if your friends are going through the same thing. If your friend is starring on a television show or is king of commercials and has plenty of money while you are scrambling to pay the rent, it is going to be harder to keep perspective about where you are in the process. It takes different people differing amounts of time to make the journey. Having friends who understand that will make it easier for all of you.

Be positive. It's one of the most important things you can do for yourself. The late actress-playwright Ruth Gordon's perspective is instructive:

✦   *Life is getting through the moment. The philosopher, William James, says to cultivate the cheerful attitude. Now nobody had more trouble than he did — except me. I had more trouble in my life than anybody. But your first big trouble can be a bonanza if you live through it. Get through the first trouble, you'll probably make it through the next one.*

> The Careerist Guide to Survival
> Paul Rosenfield
> *The Los Angeles Times*
> April 25, 1982

If you don't know anyone, get into a class or explore one of the 12-Step Groups. There's comfort for every problem from Alcoholics Anonymous to the other AA: Artists Anonymous. Even though this group is for all kinds of artists, you'll find a majority are actors and writers. There are other *A's*: NA (Narcotics Anonymous), ACA (Adult Children of Alcoholics), OA (Overeaters Anonymous), etc.

No matter who you are, there is probably a group with which you can identify, that will provide you with confidential support for free. You'll be better served if you don't look to these groups for your social life. They supply a forum where you can talk about what is bothering you, but these support groups are not your family and though helpful, they are not your best friends, either. Put energy into your personal relationships to fill those needs. You create your life. Will Rogers said, *People are about as happy as they want to be.* I agree, I believe we all get what we really want.

If you are a member of the Screen Actors Guild, Actors Equity or AFTRA, check for support groups within the unions or get involved in one of their committees. You'll have the chance to be involved in a productive activity with your peers on a regular basis that will give you a family and a focus.

Getting To Know The City

It's easy to get around the Island of Manhattan. If you are not directionally inclined, this is your chance to finally understand about north, south, east, and west. The

Hudson River is west and guess where the East River is?

You'll notice as you travel uptown (north) that the numbers get larger and as you go downtown toward Wall Street, Chinatown, and the Statue of Liberty (south) that the numbers get smaller. The numbers stop at Houston (pronounced how-ston). Then you have to deal with names.

The quickest way to get anywhere is on a bicycle if you have the courage, but that's too scary for me, so I walk. Cabs are expensive and frequently very slow. Fastest transportation is the subway. Many people don't like to use it, but I've personally never had any trouble. Subways require tokens which can also be used on buses. It makes sense to buy a supply of tokens so you don't have to stand in line each time. You can buy tokens at banks as well as the subway stations. Some stations don't have manned token booths at all times, so keep a supply in your pocket.

Instead of laying in a supply of tokens, a handy alternative is the MetroCard which accomplishes the same thing. Cards are available in amounts up to $80 and are refillable. All you have to do is swipe the card as you enter the subway. MetroCards are handy and available at some newsstands as well as at the subway station booth.

Go to any subway station or look in the front of the Manhattan phone book for a free subway map. You'll find addresses of New York theatres in the same place.

There are subways that only go up and down the East Side (Lexington Avenue) and some that only go up and down the West Side (7th Avenue) and some (the E & F) that do both. There are some that only go crosstown, at 14th Street, 42nd Street and 59th Street. Buses are great for shorter hops, but you must have exact change, a subway token or a MetroCard.

I can walk across town in about 20 minutes; you probably can, too. There used to be a great guide that an enterprising actor published listing ways to get around town without going outdoors — using subway tunnels, connecting buildings, etc. That book is long gone. If you come up with similar information, perhaps you can write your own book.

Crosstown blocks (they go east and west) are about three times as long as downtown blocks (which go north and south). It takes about the same amount of time to walk from 42nd to 59th Streets as it takes to go from Lexington Avenue to Broadway.

In the front of the phone book you'll find a guide to figuring out cross streets to numbered addresses. For instance, if you are at 1501 Broadway, you are between 43rd and 44th Streets. Tear the guide out and put it in the front of your appointment book, it will save you time and shoe leather.

I've included a map to give you an overview of Manhattan which includes the Broadway theatre district, the Public Theatre, The Theatre Library at Lincoln Center, the TKTS Booth (half-price tickets to Broadway and Off-Broadway shows), the various television networks, bookstores, etc. Here's the key:

1.   ABC Television
     1330 Avenue of the Americas
     at 54th Street

2.   Actors Equity Association (AEA)
     165 West 46th Street
     East of Broadway

3.   Actors' Studio
     432 West 44th Street
     btwn 9th & 10th Avenues

4.   AFTRA/American Federation
     of Radio & Television Artists
     260 Madison Avenue
     at 38th Street

Manhattan Map

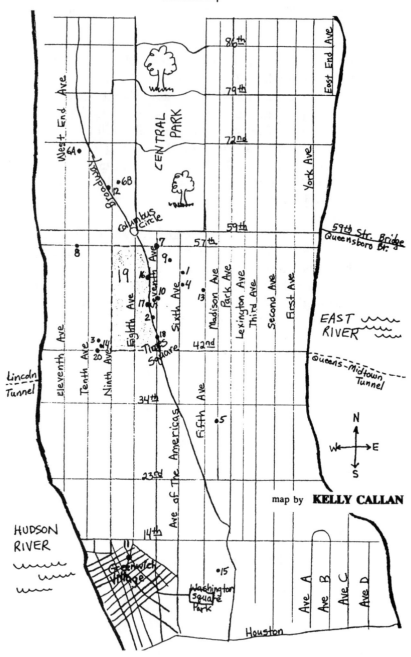

map by **KELLY CALLAN**

5. American Academy of Dramatic Arts
   120 Madison Avenue
   at 32nd Street

6. Applause Theatre Books
   211 West 71st Street
   btwn Broadway & West End Avenue

7. Carnegie Hall
   881 7th Avenue
   at 57th Street

8. CBS Television Studios
   524 West 57th Street
   btwn 10th & 11th Avenues

9. City Center
   131 West 55th Street
   btwn 6th & 7th Avenues

10. The Drama Book Shop
    723 7th Avenue
    at 48th Street, 2nd Floor

11. HB Studios
    120 Bank Street in the Village
    West of Hudson Street

12. Lincoln Center
    64th Street
    at Columbus Avenue

12. The Lincoln Center Library of Performing Arts
    40 Lincoln Center Plaza
    at 66th Street

13. NBC Television
    30 Rockefeller Plaza
    5th Avenue & 49th Street

14. Manhattan Plaza
    43rd Street
    btwn 9th & 10th Avenues

15. The Public Theatre
    425 Lafayette Street
    South of 14th Street, Broadway

16. Screen Actors Guild
    1515 Broadway
    at 44th Street

17. TKTS (Half Price Theatre Tickets)
    Duffy Square/North End of Times Square
    at 47th Street

18. Theatre District (Broadway)
    42nd to 57th Streets
    6th to 9th Avenues

19. Theatre Row
    42nd Street
    btwn 9th & 11th Avenues

Get A Job

Once you have found a place to live, it is vital for more than financial reasons to find a job.

Having a job gives form to your life. It gives you a place to go every day, a family of people to relate to and helps you feel as though you are part of the City and not a tourist. Nothing feeds depression more than sitting at home alone in a strange city. Even if you know your way around, you'll find as time goes on, that activity is the friend of the actor. Depression feeds on itself and must not be allowed to get out of hand.

If you are fortunate and tenacious enough to find a job in the business, you'll find you are not only finally in the system on some level, but that you're being paid to continue your education. There is no way in the world you can learn what it's really like to be in the business until you experience it first-hand. You'll get to spend every day with people who are interested in the same things you are. Who knows? You might not even like showbusiness when you get a closer look. Better to find out now.

If you can combine a show biz job with flexible hours permitting auditions, that's the best of all possibilities.

✦   *Always be available. Don't say you are an actor if you have a 9-5 job. If you must waitress, do it at night.*
Sharon Carry
The Carry Company Talent Representatives

As soon as you are working in the business in any category, you are in the system and on your way. I don't want to imply that coming up with one of these jobs is the easiest task in the world, but it is definitely worth the effort.

Encountering Agents

Before your resume is ready for you to be interviewing agents as possible business partners, you may find yourself encountering them either in your work or on a social level. Just as doctors don't like to listen to your symptoms at a party, an agent wants to party in peace, so be a professional and talk about something other than your career. Agents prefer to do business in their offices.

✦　*I'm not the kind of agent that's going to go up to you and say,* Who's your agent? I'm better than he is. *We're in a highly competitive business. It's bad enough already. I don't have to make it worse. I don't like people to steal my clients, so I don't steal other people's clients.*

　　　Pat House
　　　The Artists Group East

If you detect signs of interest from anyone; directors, producers, etc. Follow up on it. Ask if there is anything you can do to help with a current project.

Get Into An Acting Class

In order to find a good teacher, you'll have to do some research. You'll want to find out their background. Who did they study with? What is the caliber of their students? Has this person worked professionally? Personally, this is an important requirement for me. I want someone who has demonstrated that they know what the hell they are talking about relative not only to acting, but to professional behavior as well.

What is your dynamic with the teacher? No one can teach you to act; a teacher can only stimulate your imagination. That is the person you are looking for.

✦　*Audit classes. See the atmosphere of the class. If it seems to be an environment to stimulate healthy growth in you, then check out the technique for technique is only part of it. You want to be sure that you are going to be in a creative space, then you find out about the technique. Is this the place where I can expand? Is this a place where I can fall on my face, where they will support me in picking myself up?*

　　　Bruce Levy
　　　Bruce Levy Agency

✦　*Like anything else that you're going to invest money and time in, an actor should shop around and see what's best for him.*

See someone whose work you admire and find out who they study with and audit that class.

Jerry Kahn
Jerry Kahn, Inc.

✦ *Choose an acting class that keeps expanding you, not just your acting, but your creativity and your being. You need constant expansion. If you are not getting that or if you feel closed down, don't continue. If you feel closed down in class, that's happening to your auditions, also.*

Bruce Levy
Bruce Levy Agency

Teachers

Here is a list of well-regarded teachers in New York. Some I know personally, some are recommended by several agents I respect or of other actors whose judgment I trust. Some are more expensive than others. If I have mentioned an institution like The Actors Studio or HB, know that all teachers there are not equal. Get a list of teachers and hang out a little to see who the students are. Audit to see which teacher seems right for you. See at least three so that you can compare. If you're broke, see if you can work for tuition.

Actors Studio
American Academy of
    Dramatic Arts
William Esper
Aaron Frankel
Harold Guskin
HB Studio
Uta Hagen
Wynn Handman
Joanna Merlin
Larry Moss

Leonard Peters
Suzanne Ringrose/soaps
Sam Schacht
Jacqueline Segal
Joan See/commercials
Neil Semer/musical
    theatre
Suzanne Shepherd
Terry Shreiber
Bill Woodman/auditions
Greg Zittel

Respected Los Angeles actor-director-author Allan Miller comes to New York a few times a year for weekend classes. Check out his excellent book, *A Passion for Acting*, Dynamic Productions, 13340 Valley Vista, Sherman Oaks, CA 91423. If his style appeals to you, call (818) 907-6262 for information.

In a good class, you will begin to meet other actors and become more knowledgeable about the marketplace.

Showcases

Showcases offer visibility, experience and the ability to hone the most important skill of all: getting along with people. But, do be selective. Even if you have always wanted to do *King Lear*, the fact is that people in the business have seen the classics many times and don't find they presents actors in a manner that suggests their marketability.

✦ *I think they should try to find a showcase which presents them in a castable light, in a role that's appropriate, and that is convenient for agents to get to. You can't get me to go to Brooklyn.*

Before they invite agents, they should be very careful (and perhaps have professional advice) as to whether or not this is a worthwhile thing to invite agents to. You can sometimes engender more hostility wasting an agent's evening if it's abominable.

Phil Adelman
The Gage Group

Be realistic in your expectations. You are probably not going to get an agent as a result of a showcase, but that director will direct another play or someone in the cast may recommend you for something else. What you are doing is building your resume and beginning to work your way into the system.

If you are a preparing to study, consider one of the important theatre schools if you can afford it and if they accept you. It does make a difference. Some schools are not only significantly superior to others, but there is a group universally accepted as the most comprehensive training for young actors and whose cachet instantly alerts the antennae of employers.

Originally a collective of Schools of Professional Training for Actors referred to as the leagues, these schools offered rigorous conservatory training. The official collective no longer exists, but those schools still offer graduates who are immediately thought by buyers (casting directors, agents, producers, directors, etc.) to be the *creme de la creme* of new young actors, surely where the next Meryl Streep and Paul Newman are coming from (and did).

Here are the schools that were either in the leagues or are thought by those that matter, as the consummate place to study acting.

American Conservatory Theatre
Carey Perloff, Artistic Director
30 Grant Avenue
San Francisco, California 94108
(415) 834-3200 Extension 5

American Repertory Theatre/Loeb Drama Center
Robert Brustein, Artistic Director
Harvard University
64 Brattle Street
Cambridge, Massachusetts 02138
(617) 495-2668

Boston University
Roger Croucher, Drama Department
855 Commonwealth Avenue
Boston, Massachusetts 02215
(617) 353-3390

Carnegie Mellon/Drama Department
Elisabeth Orion
College of Fine Arts/School of Drama
Pittsburgh, Pennsylvania 15213-3890
(412) 268-2392

Catholic University of America
Department of Drama/Dr. Gitta Honegger
The Hartke Theatre
Cardinal Station
Washington, District of Columbia 20064
(202) 319-5358

Juilliard School
Kathy Hood, Director of Admissions
60 Lincoln Center Plaza
New York, New York 10023
(212) 799-5000 Extension 4

New York University/Drama Department
Arthur Bartow, Artistic Director
721 Broadway 3rd Floor
New York City, New York 10003
(212) 998-1850

North Carolina School of the Arts
Alexander Ewing
200 Waughtown Street
Winston-Salem, North Carolina 27117-2189
(910) 770-3399

Southern Methodist University/Division of Theatre
Meadows School of the Arts/Greg Poggi
P. O. Box 750356
Dallas, Texas 75275-0356
(214) 692-3217

State University of New York (at Purchase)
Israel Hicks
735 Anderson Hill Road
Purchase, New York 10577
(914) 251-6830

University of California (at San Diego)
Department of Theatre/Walt Jones
9500 Gilman Drive
La Jolla, California 92093-0344
(619) 534-6889

Yale Drama School/Yale University
Dean Stan Wojewodski, Artistic Director
222 York Street
New Haven, Connecticut 06520
(203) 432-1505

If you graduate from one of these prestigious theatre schools, you are ahead of the game as far as agents in NY/LA are concerned. And in fact, you probably will be better trained. Actors in these programs are routinely scouted by agents and sometimes procure representation as early as their freshman year. An important aspect of the education is the annual presentation by the leagues of their graduating students in a showcase produced in New York specifically for an audience of agents and casting directors.

✦ *Although the leagues may sometimes lead to auditions for immediate employment — on a soap opera, in summer stock, in an Off Broadway play — more often it serves as a casting director's mental Rolodex of actors to use in future project.*

Acting Is One Thing, Getting Hired Another
Jill Gerston
The New York Times
May 25, 1997

All of the league schools offer excellent training, but they are hard to get into and expensive, so consider carefully and have a backup. This type of education requires a big commitment of time and money. Choose the school that is right for you.

Even if you are educated at the best schools and arrive highly touted with interest from agents, ex-William Morris agent Joanna Ross told me there is still a period of adjustment:

✦ *When you come out of school, you gotta freak out for a while. And there's just not anything else that can be done about it because (particularly actors who were in very high-powered training programs) they've been working night and day doing seven different things at once and now they're suddenly out and dry and nothing. It takes a year at least, to kind of get over that and learn to be unemployed. And they have to learn to deal with that. It happens to everybody. It's not just you.*

Even if you can't make it to a league school, all is not lost:

✦ *The truth is, a great performance in the leagues can jump-start a career, but if these kids have talent, they'll get noticed. They just won't be as fast out of the starting gate...they just have to do it the old-fashioned way by pounding the pavements, reading Back-Stage, calling up friends, going to see directors they know and knocking on agents' doors.*

Acting is One Thing, Getting Hired Another
Jill Gerston
The New York Times
May 25, 1997

Assess The Marketplace

Analyzing the marketplace and using that information wisely can save you years of unfocused activity. If you were starting any other kind of business, you would expect to do extensive research to see if there was a need for the product you had decided to sell.

In addition to checking out actors, noting who is working and where, notice and keep a file on casting directors, producers, directors, and writers. Note which writers seem to be writing parts for people like you. Become an intelligent entrepreneur.

Learn and practice remembering the names of everybody. Know who the critics are. Note those whose taste agrees with yours. Think of this educational process as your Ph.D. If you want to be a force in the business, begin now to think of yourself as such and assume your rightful place. I like the definition of the word force: *energy, power, strength, vigor, vitality, impact, value, weight.*

With each new detail about the business that you ingest and have ready at your fingertips, your vitality increases. With each play you read, see, rehearse, perform in; with each writer, actor, director, casting director, costumer, etc., that you support, your power grows.

The Unions

Beginning actors unduly focus on membership in the unions. Although routinely ⅓ of the 88,000 members of Screen Actors Guild make *no money at all* in a given year (and the numbers in Equity and AFTRA are similar), actors feel that membership in the unions will change their lives.

It will. It will make you ineligible to work in any of the non-union films shooting around the city that can give you access to some film for your reel. If you are not ready to get work as a principal on a regular basis, it may not be time for you to be in the union.

Becoming a member of the union is a worthy goal. I can remember the thrill when I got my Equity card (somehow that was the card that meant you were an actor), but I was far along in my resume. Make sure you are too.

Working as an Extra

I have a bias against working as an extra if your goal is to play principal parts. It's tempting to accept extra work as a way to qualify for guild membership, pay rent, keep insurance active or get on a set. I understand that. So saying, I would like to recount a conversation I had with an agent. I asked the agent if producers wouldn't just look at an actor who does extra work and say, *Oh, but he's just an extra* and not consider him for principal work? His answer was chilling;

✦   *We all do. I spoke to a casting director the other day about an actor and that's exactly what she said.*
        The actor has to learn where to draw the line and say, okay, I can't do this anymore. *A lot of people can't. They get used to the money, used to the insurance and their resumes reflect that they are full time extras.*

This otherwise credible agent encourages actors to work as extras (after all, he is making a commission) expecting them to know when to draw the line at what is too much extra work. To me, it's like saying, *here, these drugs will make you feel better. Just take them for a while, I know you will be able to stop in time.*

It would be a lot more advantageous for you to work in some other capacity in order to pay your rent or observe the business from the inside. Become an assistant or work in production. You will see what goes on, make some money and you won't be fooling yourself into thinking you are really acting. You will be more driven to pursue work that will further your career.

Emergencies

Screen Actors Guild (SAG), Actors Equity Association (AEA) and The American Federation of Television and Radio Artists (AFTRA) all have some kind of financial assistance available to members in an emergency situation. If you are not a member of a union, talk to your acting teacher and ask for advice.

There are also many city agencies equipped to deal with people in need. There is low-cost counseling available through the city of New York and through the Schools of Psychology of some universities. Call the schools or look in the front of the white pages of the phone book for information.

Invaluable Publications

Ross Reports Television (commonly called *The Ross Report)* is a monthly that prints names and addresses of agents, casting directors, networks, unions and advertising agencies as well as other helpful information. It's not necessary to buy it monthly, changes don't happen that often, but if you are not in regular touch with a specific group of agents, get a new copy every three months or so. *The Ross Report* is sold at The Drama Book Shop plus most good newsstands and available directly from the publisher:

Television Index, Inc.
40-29 27th Street
Long Island City, NY 11101
(718) 937-3990

Backstage and *ShowBusiness* are weekly showbiz newspapers that detail theatre, film and television information of every kind. Available at most newsstands.

The Players Guide is an annual reference guide routinely used by casting directors, agents and producers to jog their memories, check for actor's agent affiliation and/or find a new face. The *Guide* is a potent tool for actors who are already in the union. It costs $100 for the first listing, less for subsequent listings, if you don't change your picture or text. You supply the money, a picture and union verification.

Get on the mailing list for the next *Guide* by calling 212-302-9474. You will have to sign a legal document saying you are in one of the performer unions. This is not something to lie about since casting directors consult the guide looking for union actors. If a casting director calls you from the book and you are not in the union, you could be sued, but if you are a member of the union and ready to book, you should be listed.

We are all embarked on an exciting adventure. Some of us are further down the road than others. It's important to enjoy the journey. From the perspective of time, I look at my life and realize that the times of great struggle were frequently the most rewarding. I also recognize that every time I work, I still learn something new — mostly about getting along with people.

When we are employed, we feel as though we will never be *un*employed again. We will. When we are not working we feel as though we will never work again. We will. What goes up must come down and vice-versa. Learn to value the ride.

Wrap Up

Personal Resources

✓ support group
✓ family
✓ teachers

Geographical Resources

✓ phone books
✓ maps
✓ NYC Convention Bureau

Professional Resources

✓ job in business
✓ acting class/teachers
✓ theatrical publications

4 Kinds of Representation

Assuming you have your life in a fairly balanced state — have an apartment, are in class, have accumulated some credits, are involved with other actors and have analyzed the marketplace in a meaningful way — it's time to confront the next hurdle. What kind of relationship do you want with your agent?

Freelance/Exclusive

Any sane person would want to know a potential business partner well before turning his business over to him. Therefore, signing with the first agent you meet is not a wise business decision for either of you. If the agent is willing, it's appropriate to enter into a freelance arrangement in which both parties are clearly considering possible future commitment.

✦ *Some people are better off not signing, possibly because they're the kind of actors that agents will only submit from time to time. The agent may not feel that that actor is very marketable and feels he doesn't want to really work hard for him.*
Jerry Kahn
Jerry Kahn, Inc.

✦ *New York is much more of a signed town than it used to be. If you are going to have a career, you really should settle on someone because freelance is not the way to go. You don't get pushed, you don't get submitted for that many things and there is no development done, let alone any marketing.*
Gary Krasny
The Krasny Office

In New York it is possible to have several different agents submitting you for projects. The beauty of this freelance arrangement is that not everyone sees you in the same way, so although one agent might not think of you for a particular job, another might.

The downside is that you must spend time agenting yourself to various agents much as you would if you were represented by a large conglomerate: staying in touch, keeping them informed of your activities, keeping your face in front of several different agencies instead of concentrating on just one.

In order to submit a freelance actor's name for a project, Screen Actors Guild rules require the agent to clear the submission with the actor. If you aren't home, if the line is busy or you're in the shower, it's possible the agent will have to send in his list without your name.

There are agents you may feel don't have enough credibility to consider signing with, but if they submit you and you connect with a job, that's good for both of you.

A negative aspect of freelance representation is that there is an absence of mutual career planning. Actors and agents with no real career potential may be happy with unfocused goals. Will you?

It's always better to have a plan. You can change it later if need be, but a goal moves you forward by its existence. Target several agents until you get a feel for who you like. That's what they are doing.

✦   *I don't sign anyone on just meeting them because I think it's a relationship. You can liken it to a marriage. There are people who might look across the street, see someone, fall madly in love, get married and live happily ever after. Sometimes it happens that way, but very rarely.*

Usually, it's the type of thing where people have to get to know each other, compare goals, compare needs and see how they work best with each other. So a freelance relationship with a client is the first step towards an exclusive relationship.

I would rather work with someone freelance for a year until we both knew it was right to sign and then be signed for the next 30 years than sign somebody right away and six months later, break the contract. You put so much emotion into it and are so involved in it that it's better to let it build until you know it's right. The freelance relationship builds to the exclusive relationship.

Flo Rothacker
DGRW

✦   *Sometimes actors don't really consider all the work an agent may do for them that doesn't result in an appointment. The agent may have said your name many times to the casting director until the CD has heard it often enough that he begins to think you are actually working.*

At that point, the actor happens to call the casting director himself and ends up with an appointment and subsequently a job. Now he calls his agent and says, Well, hey. I got the job myself. Why should I play you commission?

In my head, I'm going, Who sat down with you and told you how to dress? Who helped you select the photos you are using right now that got you that audition? Who helped you texture your resume? Who introduced you to the casting director? What makes you think you did that on your own?

They don't see it. They don't see that like a manager, I have taken them from here to here. They've always had an audition for it. What makes them think they got this on their own?

Most actors don't realize the initial investment we make, the time, the energy, the phone calls, the mail, the hours collecting and preparing and getting them to the right places. There is no compensation for that until maybe two years down the road. At that point, you've made them so good that someone else signs them anyway.

There's not a lot of loyalty among actors. They'll always want the person who gets them the next job. They don't comprehend what we go through to get them ready for that point where they can get job.

H. Shep Pamplin
Oppenheim-Christie

A signed relationship with the right theatrical agent is a worthy goal. Don't be so afraid of making the right choice that you make no choice. Being signed can make your life a lot easier.

The agent makes his choice based on his thinking that you will work and help him pay his rent if he submits you for the right projects.

Once you and an agent choose each other, it is easier to stay in touch and become a family. It behooves you to put a lot of energy into the relationship so that the agent does think of you. If you are signed and your agent doesn't think of you, there are no other agents down the line to fall back on.

If you are smart, you won't give up your own agenting efforts just because you are signed, you'll just focus them differently. Too many actors sign and sit back waiting for the agent to take over all the professional details of their lives. The more you can do to help your agent, the better off both of you will be.

Theatrical vs. Commercial Representation

Resume expectations of commercial agents are quite different than those of theatrical agents. Although this book is focused on agents who submit actors for theatre, film and television, I would like to discuss one particular aspect of the commercial agent/actor relationship that relates to theatrical representation.

Some agencies have franchises only with SAG and AFTRA that do not cover commercials. Some agencies have no franchises with SAG and AFTRA that cover actors for film and/or television. Some agents have everything.

Because commercials are so lucrative (and theatre is not), some agents require your name on the dotted line on a commercial contract before they will submit you theatrically. If that is the deal someone offers you, be wary. If they have confidence in their ability to get you work in the theatrical venue, they will not require commercial participation.

Many actors who are successful in commercials

Many actors who are successful in commercials find it difficult to cross over into theatre, film, and television and sign joint agreements only to find that they are never submitted with the agency's theatrical clients.

Commercial vs. Theatrical Success

Frequently, commercial progress comes swiftly and the actor finds he hasn't had opportunities to build the same credibility on the theatrical level as he has commercially. He doesn't realize the agent does not feel comfortable sending him on theatrical calls because of the disparity between his theatrical and commercial resume. Until the actor addresses this, signing across the board is not a good business decision. There are many reasons, not the least of which is the contractual commitment.

In the rules of the Screen Actors Guild, if an actor has had no work in 91 days, he can void his contract with an agent simply by sending a letter to the agent plus copies to all unions advising them of Paragraph 6 (See Glossary).

If you have been working commercially, but are not sent out theatrically, you might want to find a new theatrical agent, but since you have been making money in commercials, you cannot utilize Paragraph 6 to end your relationship. Consider carefully the commitment you are making when you sign. You may have heard about actors who got out of their contracts easily, but I also know actors who had to buy their way out of their contract with a large financial settlement.

On the other hand, if you have a successful theatrical career going and no commercial representation and your theatrical agent has commercial credibility and wants to sign you, why not allow him to make some realistic money by taking your commercial calls?

People win commercials because they are blessed with the commercial look of the moment. It's easy to get cocky when you are making big commercial money and conclude that you are farther along in your career than you are. What you really are is momentarily rich. Keep things in perspective. Thank God for the money and use it to take classes from the best teachers in town so that you can begin to build theatrical credibility.

It's possible to cultivate some theatrical casting directors on your own. A few are accessible. When you have done a prestigious showcase or managed to accumulate film through your own efforts with casting directors, theatrical agents will be more interested.

It's all a process.

Wrap Up

Freelance

✓   gives actor other submission possibilities
✓   requires more upkeep
✓   requires vigilant phone monitoring
✓   gives you a chance to get to know the agent
✓   no over-all game plan

Exclusive

✓   more focused representation
✓   all your eggs are in one basket
✓   easier to have a close relationship
✓   easy to get lazy

Theatrical vs. Commercial Representation

✓   more financial rewards for commercial success
✓   all representation at same agency can block Paragraph 6 protection
✓   takes different credits for theatrical credibility

5   What Everybody Wants

If you could sign with any agent in town, which one would you choose? Would ICM be right for you? Could J. Michael Bloom be the answer? Maybe you would be better off with The Gage Group? All of the agencies I just mentioned are prestigious, but that doesn't necessarily mean acquiring A instead of B would be a wise career move.

Before we start looking for the ultimate agent or agents, consider what agents are looking for.

The Definitive Client

✦   *I want to know either that they work and make a lot of money so I can support my office or that the potential to make money is there. I am one of the people who goes for talent, so I do take people who are not big moneymakers, because I am impressed with talent.*

> Martin Gage
> *The Gage Group*

Beverly Anderson told me an instructive story about her reaction to meeting a prospective client:

✦   *Sigourney Weaver asked to come in and meet me when she was with a client of mine in Ingrid Bergman's show,* The Constant Wife. *She's almost six feet tall. I'm very tall myself* and when I saw her, I thought, God, honey, you're going to have a tough time in this business because you're so huge. *And she floated in and she did something no one had ever done. She had this big book with all her pictures from Bryn Mawr or Radcliffe of things she had done and she opened this book and she comes around and drapes herself over my shoulders from behind my chair and points to herself in these pictures. She was hovering over me and I thought,* No matter what happens with me, this woman is going to make it. *There was*

determination and strength and self-confidence and positiveness. Nobody's ever done that to me before.
>Beverly Anderson
>*Beverly Anderson Agency*

Weaver's strength comes, in some portion, from having a strong, successful father, Pat Weaver, producer of *The Today Show*. Though many of us were not blessed with such an effective role model, it's possible and wise to pick someone who is living the life you want, study them and use some of their methods in pursuit of your goal.

Weaver was also blessed with a top drawer education, another valuable asset:

✦   *Training is the most important thing. I get very annoyed with people. Someone is attractive, so people say,* You should be in television, *and then the actor thinks that's just going to just happen.*
>J. Michael Bloom
>*J. Michael Bloom*

If you want to be pursued by an agent, find out what qualities catch an agent's eye. The late Michael Kingman was one of New York's most insightful and successful agents, he was quite articulate about what attracted him to actors:

✦   *His talent. To be moved. To laugh. Feelings. Somebody who has contagious emotions.*
I'm looking for actors with talent and health, mental health and the ability to say, It's my career and I devote my life to this. *It's an attitude, not a spoken thing. It's an attitude that* today is not the last day of my life.

Didn't Michael realize that if we had mental health we probably would not need to be actors?

✦   *I'm looking for an actor with the ability to get a job and pay me a commission. I'm looking for people who are gorgeous and don't stutter. I'm looking for people who already have credits I can use so I can sell them.*

Beverly Anderson
Beverly Anderson Agency

✦   *The people we work with best are actors who are committed to their craft and are willing to do regional theater as well as off Broadway and Broadway as well as film and television.*

The focus should be on training and growing yourself. Experiencing life so you can bring that to a character and to a performance. The interview part of the audition is just as important as the audition. Who you are as a person, as well as who you are as an actor.

Jim Flynn
Berman, Boals and Flynn, Inc.

✦   *Spark. Personality that jumps up and says,* I'm alive. *There's a personality that comes out.*

Mary Sames
Sames & Rollnick

✦   *In younger clients, I'm looking for marketability, along with a centeredness, a groundedness in where they are right now, that they know where they are at this particular point in time — which is going to change tenfold as they grow.*

I look at training. Most of my young clients are sent to me from independent films or I get them out of the top league schools.

I look for a young person who sort of has an idea of who they are right now because it's a really tough ride.

Meg Mortimer

✦   *I'm drawn to actors who I feel are talented and have a commitment to win. I'll go through anything with an actor as long as his commitment is to win.*

Bruce Levy
Bruce Levy Agency

✦   *A spark. Something that's unusual. Usually from a performance. But, they can cool my interest by their behavior at our interview. You not only have to have the talent, you have to apply it. You can tell sometimes by the responses that they don't yet have that capacity to apply it.*

It always boils down to the talent. If somebody has a talent even though it's someone who's a drunk, you know that there's still the wonderful performance to be gotten. On the other hand, you must ask, Is it worth going through all that to wait for that wonderful performance?

Jeff Hunter
William Morris Agency

✦   *Talent. And a resume that speaks for itself. It talks to me. I look at the places that you have worked, for a strong classical background. Where did you train? Yale? Juilliard? I hate to say it, but it makes a difference. It will open doors for you.*

Mary Sames
Sames & Rollnick

✦   *I like to work with people that I like as well as respect. I like to work with people who are fairly sane, fairly stable, certainly dependable, who are well-trained and who have talent. A great deal of that can be communicated in the personal projection of the person.*

Pat House
The Artists Group East

✦   *I want clients to come to me prepared. To have a sense of who they are, the kind of career they're likely to have, good self-knowledge, good reality about themselves.*

Phil Adelman
The Gage Group

✦   *If they're older and have been in the business and don't have some career going, it's harder because they're now going to be up against people who have so many more and important credits.*

Robert Malcolm
The Artists Group East

✦   *Since we are own bosses, we can choose who we want to work with. When a client approaches and we get even an inkling that this is going to be a high maintenance client, we don't choose them.*

Jim Flynn
Berman, Boals and Flynn, Inc.

✦   *I like performers who see themselves clearly, who have clear ideas of who they are, what they can do and I like them to be responsive to comments, criticism and advice borne of having done this since 1949. Period.*

Fifi Oscard
Fifi Oscard Associates, Inc.

✦   *When you talk about clients who are older, I prefer actors whose work I have followed and admired. People whose careers excite me.*

Meg Mortimer

✦   *I like clients that challenge me as an agent, as they are not easily typable. I think they end up having more range. Although it may be more difficult sometimes to get them seen, it's more rewarding because it's more creative for you as an agent. If you look at my list, you would notice that I tend to choose actors who aren't very* straight on.

Peter Strain
Peter Strain & Associates / Los Angeles

✦   *I love those actors who are always trying to further perfect their craft by always being in class. Because of that, they always seem to be in the mainstream of working actors because they're so serious about it.*

Monty Silver
Silver, Massetti & Szatmary, East Ltd.

What To Look For In An Agent

✦   *One of the chief factors that determines the value of an agent is the amount of information that he has available to him. It is impossible for a small agent to possess the amount of information that a large agency can. We track hundreds of projects weekly at all of the studios and networks. If a client walks in and asks about a project, I can haul out 400 pages of notes and say,* Oh yeah, it's at this studio and this is the producer and they're doing a rewrite right now and they're hoping to go with it on this date and talking to so and so about it. *I have that information.*

Gene Parseghian
William Morris Agency

✦ *If you have a choice, look hard for someone you can really trust and someone who is not sycophantic. Someone who will say to you:* You were not good last night. *Most agents won't tell you because they are afraid you will leave them. You have got to have someone you can trust. I think that when you get that person, you should trust them. I think if they give you advice and say,* Don't do this *or,* Do this, *you should listen to them. The agent should be trusted for his expertise. If you were going to have brain surgery and you asked the surgeon what he was going to do, you wouldn't say,* Well, no. I don't think you should do it that way. *You would say,* Well, okay. I'm in your hands. *You should trust until such time as you cannot trust the person, then that is the time to make a change.*

Lionel Larner
Lionel Larner, Ltd.

Make sure you are practical in your assessment of your agent's ability to produce auditions. Actors sometime grade their agents by the number of auditions they get them out on not the quality or appropriateness. If you're not being sent on projects that you are right for, all those auditions are just for show. Former agent, Marvin Starkman has a realistic perspective:

✦ *If the actor/agent relationship were based on getting auditions for everything, then the agent would have a right to say that you must get everything he sends you out on. If you don't get everything he sends you on, then you have a one-sided relationship.*

Kind of puts it where it is, doesn't it?

Vision/Goals

If the actor and the agent are not on the same wave-length, there can be no way to communicate.

✦   *I had a funny looking lady come in, mid 30s, chubby, not very pretty. For all I know, this woman could be brilliant. I asked her what roles she could play, what she thought she should get. She saw herself playing Winona Ryder's roles. I could have been potentially interested in this woman in the areas in which she could work. But it was a turnoff, because not only do I know that she's not going after the right things so she's not preparing correctly but she's not going to be happy with the kinds of things I'm going to be able to do for her. So I wouldn't want to commit to that person.*

> Phil Adelman
> *The Gage Group*

✦   *The actor should look at the agent's client list to see if he fits in there. He should look at the agent's integrity and background. He should look for communication.*

> Meg Mortimer

✦   *What's essential is that the goals the actor sets for himself and what the agent wants for the actor be the same. Or at the very least, compatible, but probably the same.*

If an actor walks in and I think that actor can be a star next month and the actor doesn't, it ain't gonna happen. If the actor thinks he's gonna be a star next month and I don't, it ain't gonna happen. By that, I mean it's not gonna work between us. Even though a great deal of it may be unspoken, there has to be a shared perspective.

> Gene Parseghian
> *William Morris Agency*

Size

A key aspect to consider in overall agent effectiveness is size. When we speak of size in relation to agents, we are speaking of his client list, the number of actors the agent has committed to represent exclusively.

One person cannot effectively represent a hundred people. It's like going to the store and buying everything you see. You can't possibly *use* everything, you're just taking it out of circulation.

It may feed your ego to be signed (*I have an agent!*), but if you are not signed with a credible agent, you may just be taking yourself out of the marketplace. Better to wait until you have the credits to support getting a better agent then to sign with someone who can't represent you effectively.

Many agents believe a good ratio is one agent to 20 to 25 clients. An agency with four agents can do well by 100 or even 140 clients, but that really is the limit. Look closely at any lists that are extravagantly over this size. It's easy to get lost on a large list.

It's all very well to have stamina, discern talent, have a short list, and be a great salesman. I take that as a given, but there are two other attributes that separate the contenders from the also-rans.

Access And Stature

The dictionary defines the word access as *ability to approach* or *admittance*.

Since the conglomerate agencies have many stars on their lists, they have plenty of ability to approach, because if the studios, networks and producers do not return their phone calls, they might find the agency retaliating by withholding their important stars.

Stature on the other hand is different entirely. Webster defines the word as *level of achievement.*

Thus, Phil Adelman and Richard Astor certainly have more stature than some beginning agent at William Morris, but because Adelman and Astor don't have an equal number of bankable stars, they might not have as much access. Get both stature and access if you can, but if you have to choose, go with access.

The central issue is, how do you choose the agent who will provide the opportunity for you to be gainfully employed in the business?

Wrap Up

The Ideal Client

✓ has talent
✓ possesses contagious emotions
✓ displays a singular personality
✓ exhibits professionalism
✓ manifests self-knowledge
✓ shows drive
✓ is innately likeable
✓ maintains mental health
✓ is well-trained
✓ boasts a good resume

The Ideal Agent

✓ is aggressive
✓ has stature
✓ has access
✓ is enthusiastic
✓ shares the actor's career vision
✓ has optimum actor/agent ratio
✓ has integrity

6 Research & Follow-through

Unfortunately, agents do not send out resumes in search of clients. Even if they are looking for clients (and they are all looking for the client who will make them wealthy and powerful beyond their dreams), agents don't send out a list of their training, accomplishments and/or a personality profile.

Beyond their list of clients (which is not, by the way, posted on their door), there is no obvious key to their worth; therefore, it is up to you to conduct an investigation of your possible business partners.

You have taken your first step. You bought this book. I have already done a lot of research for you by interviewing agents, asking about their background, looking at their client lists, interviewing some of their clients, and in general engaging in conversations with anyone and everyone in the business who might have something informed to say about theatrical agents. I've also read everything that I could get my hands on regarding agents and the way the business is conducted.

You should begin to have agent conversations with everyone in the business with whom you come in contact. If you are just beginning in the business and your contacts are limited to your peers, they will probably be just as uninformed as you. Never mind, ask anyway. You never know where information lurks.

As I said in the Introduction, read this entire book before you make any judgments about your readiness to attract an agent or what kind of agent you seek. Your understanding of various bits of data is enhanced by an informed overview, so resolve to have one. Make sure you have absorbed how the business really works, what you have a right to expect from an agent, what you can realistically expect of an agent, and what your contribution is to the mix.

Prepare yourself as an artist and as a business

person so that you can operate on the level to which you aspire. If your work and presentation are careless, what kind of agent is going to want you?

Get On With It

After you've digested this book completely, go back and read the agency listings again and take notes. You'll learn their lineage, education, credits (clients), the size of their list and get some idea of their style. If there is someone who interests you, check the index to see if the agent is quoted elsewhere in the book. Those quotes can give you additional clues as to how the agent conducts business, views the world, and how comfortable you might feel with him.

If you read his dossier and don't recognize any of the clients' names, that may mean his clients are respected working actors whose names you don't happen to know or they could be up-and-coming actors who have not yet worked. You can only evaluate the agent accurately if you know exactly what his list means. If he only works freelance, that tells you something, too.

If the only clients the agent has on his list are stars and you are just beginning, that agent is too far along for you. If the agent has bright-looking actors with no important credits, he is building his list. If you fit that category of client, perhaps you and the agent can build credibility together. It's worth a shot.

If you are an actor of stature, you will be looking for an agent that lists some of your peers. Some fine agencies have opened in the last two or three years whose names may not be as well-known as older agencies, but who have real credibility. Usually these are started by agents who interned at larger offices, learned the business, groomed some clients, and left the nest (frequently with some of the agency's choicest clients) to open their own agencies.

Once you have a list of agents who have caught your attention, go to Screen Actors Guild, Actors

Equity or American Federation of Television and Radio Artists and spend an afternoon leafing through the pages of *The Academy Players Directory* or *The Players Guide* raising your consciousness by noticing the names and faces of clients of particular agents. Names of actors might not be enough, faces will be more revealing. Notice which agents represent the actors in your peer group. This will help you create your agent wish list.

The Screen Actors Guild maintains a current listing of agencies and their client lists. If you are a member of The Screen Actors Guild, you have access to this material. Go by and check out the current client lists of the agents that interest you. There is a code to identify the size of the list and whether the clients are signed theatrically or commercially. If you have access to both SAG lists and *The Players Guide* and/or *The Academy Players Directory*, check everything.

TPG and *APD* have actors listed alphabetically. The SAG list indexes agents alphabetically showing size of list and names of clients. It's easier to get a focused picture of a particular agency looking at the SAG agency lists than looking at lots of pictures in *TPG*.

As your research continues, you will have fantasies about the large conglomerate agencies. Check out Chapter 9, Star/Conglomerate Agencies before you form your final opinion. There are many pros and cons to representation by star agencies at various levels of one's career.

While you are salivating about life at ICM, consider that most stars come to celebrity agencies after a struggling independent agent helped the actor achieve enough stature and access of his own that the conglomerate agent felt his interest was financially justified.

William Morris, ICM, CAA and United Talent do not offer career-building services. The large corporations are there to cash in on the profits. Although it is true that star representation enhances some careers, it is not true in all cases.

In making your agent selections, make sure you

are seeking an agent you have the credits to attract: Noah Wylie's agent is probably not going to be interested. Make sure clients on the agent's list are your peers. It's all very well and good to think big, but you must walk before you run.

Don't expect an agent who has spent years building his credibility to be interested in someone who just got off the bus. Remember, you must effectively agent yourself until you are at a point that a credible agent will give you a hearing.

I met a young actor some years ago who had just arrived in California. Because he had lots of chutzpah, he was able to hustle a meeting with an agent far above him in stature. The agent asked if there was an audition tape available. Although he had none, the actor said his tape was in New York and that he would send for it. He kept putting the agent off and finally volunteered to do a scene in the agent's office. He ended up getting signed. After he was signed, he confessed there was no tape.

A year and no jobs later, the actor angrily left the agent in search of another agent. It still has not occurred to the actor that he was just not ready for representation on that level.

I'm sure he will manage to waste even more time before it occurs to him to spend energy studying and doing plays instead of squandering it trying to trick an inappropriate agent into signing him.

✦ *I feel sorry for the people who spend all their time trying to use various forms of manipulation to get an agent while their contemporaries are working and learning. And the ones working at working will rise right up. The people who were assuming it's some kind of game will disappear.*
Fifi Oscard
Fifi Oscard Agency, Inc.

Who Do You Love?

At this point, you should have some idea of which agents appeal to you. Some names will keep coming up. Make a list. Even if you know you are only interested in Philip Carlson or Bill Timms, target at least five names. You can't intelligently make a choice unless you have something to compare. You don't know that you like Agent A best unless you have seen Agent B and Agent C.

It's time to ask advice from casting directors with whom you have formed relationships. A CD who has hired you will probably be pleased that you asked his opinion. Tell him you are agent shopping and that you would like to run a few names by him.

Also ask for any names he might like to add to your list. Listen to the casting director's opinion but remember, he has a far different relationship with an agent than you will have. Make your own decision.

At this point your research is based on style, stature, access, size of list, word of mouth and fantasy. Let's forge ahead to face-to-face encounters.

Getting A Meeting

The best way to contact anyone is through a referral. If you know someone on the agent's list who will act as a go-between, this is good. If a casting director whose advice you have sought offers to call, this is better, but don't put the CD on the spot by asking. If you ask for advice about agents and he feels comfortable recommending you, he will suggest it. If he doesn't, be thankful for the advice.

Winning an Academy Award, a Tony, or an Emmy is, of course, a great door opener. What else?

If you are young and beautiful, just go drop your picture off in person (mid-week, late afternoon) looking as Y&B as possible. It is sad (for the rest of us) but true, that if you are really Y&B and can speak at all, few will require that you do much more. May as well cash in on it.

If you are smart, you will study while cashing in since Y&B doesn't linger long and you may want to work in those grey years of your 30s and beyond.

You're not Y&B? Me neither. So this is what I suggest:

If you are just starting in the business or you don't have any strong credits, concentrate on classes. Join theatre groups, get involved with showcases. View as much theatre, film and television as possible.

Notice names of directors and writers as well as actors. Begin making a list of the people you would like to work with. Align yourself with peers whose work you respect. Form a group that includes actors, writers and directors and focus on furthering each other's careers by working together.

Join groups of writers and directors like Independent Features Projects. Make yourself available to read scripts or work in independent films. New York is the capital of the independent film movement. Check out the film school at New York University and see if you can leave a picture and resume.

Don't approach agents and/or casting directors asking for meetings until you build up your resume and have something to show them.

If you have graduated from one of the league schools and/or have some decent credits and/or an Audition Tape (Glossary), and have a clear idea how you should be marketed, it's time to begin.

Send a letter preceding the picture and resume by a couple of days. Letters get read; pictures and resumes tend to sit on the *whenever I get to it stack.*

Make sure your letter is typed on good stationery. The feel of expensive paper in one's hands makes an unconscious impression that the writer is to be taken seriously. State that you are interested in representation. Say that you are impressed with the agent's client list (make sure you know who is on it) and that your credits compare favorably. If you have a particularly impressive credit, mention it.

I've been asked to provide an example. Please don't use it verbatim or every agent in town will get identical letters. This is just to stimulate your thinking:

Dear Mary Smith:

I've just moved to New York from Timbuktu and am interested in representation. I have spoken to George Brown and Sheila Jones who are in my acting class. We are all studying with Jacqueline Segal. They have told me that they have worked through you.

Since I am in their peer group, I thought I might fit in with your client list. Although I am new to town, I do have a few credits. I met John Casting Director and have worked two jobs through him: *Hello Everyone* and *It Pays to Study*. The parts were small, but it was repeat business and everyone has to start somewhere. I'm compiling an audition tape.

My picture and resume will be in your office by Thursday. I'll call on Friday to see if you have a few minutes and might be interested in seeing my audition tape. I'm looking forward to meeting you.

Sincerely,
Hopeful Actor

I was told by an agent recently that the best way to get an agent to notice your picture is to walk it in. Don't chat up the receptionist, just deliver the picture in a manila envelope addressed to a specific agent with a note inside. He told me that pictures that end up on a desk delivered by hand usually pique interest.

✦ *Most actors send their pictures out over the weekend and they all come in on Monday and Tuesday. If you sent yours on Wednesday and it arrived on a Friday, it might be the only one on the agent's desk.*
Peter Beilin
Peter Beilin Agency, Inc.

If you've just graduated from one of the league schools, mention this and some roles you have played. Make sure your picture and resume tell the truth and arrive when you promised them.

If your letter has stirred interest, your picture will be opened immediately. Call the day after your picture arrives. When you call (late afternoon is best), be up and be brief. Be a person the agent wants to talk to. If he doesn't want a meeting, get over the disappointment and get on to the next agent on your list.

Try to set up meetings with at least three agents and plan all the details of the meeting.

For starters, be on time and look terrific. This is a job interview, after all. Choose clothing that makes you feel good and look successful, and that suggests you take pride in yourself. Bright colors not only make people remember you, but they usually make you feel good, too. Remember, in today's world, packaging is at least as important as product.

Go in and act like yourself. Be natural and forthright. Don't bad-mouth other agents. If you are leaving another agent, don't get into details about why you are leaving. If the agent asks, just say it wasn't working out.

Agents are all members of the same fraternity. Unless this agent is stealing you away from someone else, he will be at least a little anxious about why you are leaving. If you bad-mouth another agent, the agent is wondering — subconsciously, at least — what you will say about *him*.

In general, don't talk too much. Give yourself a chance to get comfortable. Adjust to the environment. Notice the surroundings. Comment on them. Talk about the weather. Talk about the stock market, the basketball game or the last play you saw. That's a great topic. It gives you each a chance to check out the other's taste.

Don't just agree with him. Say what you think.

If you hated it, just say it just didn't work for you. Remember, this is a first date. You are both trying to figure out if you are interested in each other.

If you've seen one of his clients in something and liked it, say so. Don't be afraid to ask questions. But use common sense.

✦ *Be careful. It's not what you ask, it's how you ask it.*
Harry Packwood
Harry Packwood Talent

Phrase questions in a positive vein. Discuss casting directors that you know and have worked for. Ask what casting directors the office has ties with. Tell the agent what your plans are. Mention the kind of roles that you feel you are ready for and that you feel you have the credits to support. Ask what he thinks. Are you on the same wavelength? Don't just send out, make sure you are also receiving.

Find out how the office works. If you are being interviewed by the owner and there are other agents, ask the owner if he will be representing you personally. Many owners are not involved in agenting on a day-to-day basis.

Find out office policy about phone calls. Are you welcome to call? Does the agent want feedback after each audition? What's the protocol for dropping by? Will they consistently view your work? Will they consult with you before turning down work? Explore your feelings about these issues before the meeting.

If you need to be able to speak to your agent regularly, now's the time to talk about it. Does the office have a policy of regularly requesting audition material for their actors at least a day in advance of the audition? Let him know what you require to be at your best. If these conversations turn the agent off, better to find out now. This is the time to assess the chemistry between the two of you.

*✦   What makes a good agent? Partially the chemistry that
goes on between an actor and an agent and partially the chemistry
that goes on between the agent and the casting director; that they
can communicate on an intelligent, non-whining wavelength. A
good agent has to be able to not be so restricted by casting
information and The Breakdown, so boxed in by what they read
that they don't expand the possibilities. And finally, that they can
get people appointments for good work.*

Marvin Starkman/Producer

During the meetings, be alert for those
intangible signs that tell you about a person. Note how
he treats his employees, whether he really listens, his
body language, how he is with people on the phone.
How do you feel when he's speaking to you? What's the
subtext?

The agent will want to know the casting
directors with whom you have relationships. Make sure
this material is at your fingertips so that you can
converse easily and intelligently. Even if your specialty is
playing dumb blondes your agent will feel more
comfortable about making a commitment to a person
who is going to be an informed business partner.

*✦   Morgan Fairchild came in, and out of the hundreds and
hundreds of actresses and actors that I have seen and had appointments with, I've never been literally interviewed by an actress:*
Okay, What have you done? Where are you going?
*Incredible. She interviewed me. Yes, I was turned off to a degree,
but I was so impressed by her brilliant mind and her smarts that I
thought to myself,* Gal, even without me, you're going to go
very far. *She came in here and she knew where she was going
and she interviewed me and I thought,* That's fantastic.

Beverly Anderson
Beverly Anderson

Beverly points to an important truth. Although
she was a little turned off by Fairchild's approach, she
saw it as a tool for success. If you want an agent to want

you, it's like any other relationship, you can't be desperate. It's important to be respectful, but don't genuflect.

✦ *When you finally get your meeting with the agent, you can't sit there and tremble and be intimidated, that's your time to impress.*
Lionel Larner
Lionel Larner, Ltd.

Now that you have met the agent, given focus to him and his accomplishments, office and personnel, impressed him with your straight-forwardness, drive, punctuality, resume, appearance, and grasp of the business and your place within it, it is time for you to close the meeting. Make it clear that you are having such a good time you could stay all day, but you realize that he is busy and that you just have time to make your voice lesson. It doesn't matter where you are going. Just have a real appointment to go to and leave.

Suggest that you both think about the meeting for a day or two and set a definite time for when you will get back to him or vice-versa. If he asks if you are meeting other agents, be truthful. If he's last on your list, mention that you need to go home and digest all the information. He will probably have to have a meeting with his staff before making a decision. Let him know you were pleased with the meeting. Even if it was not your finest moment — or his — be gracious. After all, you both did your best.

My advice is to hurry home and write down all your feelings about the meeting and put them away for 24 hours. Then write your feelings down again and compare them. When I was interviewing agents for this book, I found I would have signed with almost any of them on the spot. They are all salesmen and they were all charming. The next day I had more perspective. By then, the hyperbole seemed to have drifted out of my head and I was able to discern more clearly what had gone on.

If the agent said he would get in touch with you and he doesn't, leave it. There are others on your list. If he forgot you, do you want him as your agent? If he is rejecting you, don't insist he do it to your face.

Remember, you are choosing an agent. The qualities you look for in a pal are not necessarily the qualities you desire in an agent.

If you want an agent on a higher level who does not seem interested, don't be deterred; there are many other agents on that level. If they all turn you down, then perhaps you are not as far along as you think. Don't be depressed, that just means you need to do more work on yourself until you are ready for those agents. If you feel you really must have representation at this time, you may need to pursue an agent on a lower level, but let's think positive.

◆   *There are clients I don't want to work with, not because they are not talented, but because I don't want to be in a constant relationship with them. They're not bad or good, they may be wonderful people, but it's not a good marriage. There is a better agent for them. You have to be able to feel you want to see it through the ups and downs, it's just personality. What's good for me might not be good for somebody else and vice-versa.*

Bruce Levy
Bruce Levy Agency

Making The Decision

I heard a story once about Mike Nichols. He was giving a speech to the actors on opening night:

Just go out there and have a good time. Don't let it worry you that The New York Times *is out there, every important media person in the world is watching you, that we've worked for days and weeks and months on this production, that the investors are going to lose their houses if it doesn't go well, that the writer will commit suicide and that it will be the end of your careers if you make one misstep. Just go out there and have a good time.*

I think that's the way many of us feel about choosing an agent. When I was in New York, I freelanced much longer than was career-appropriate because I was afraid of making a wrong decision that could have irrevocable consequences on my career.

✦ *I find that actors are sometimes overly cautious. They are sometimes guided by anxiety or fear and that leads one to say,* No, I'm going to wait, *when there is nothing to lose by signing with a particular agent who is interested. If it doesn't work, the actor can always get out of it. It's only for a year, anyway. There is so much more that can be done when there is an effective responsible agent at work that sometimes it's an actor's insecurity that holds him back, and I think wrongly so.*
Gene Parseghian
William Morris Agency

There are some agents who do not share Gene's feelings. Many would rather not sign you if they feel you are not ready for a long-term commitment.

✦ *I've had actors I was freelancing with say to me,* I'm going with, *I don't know,* Fifi Oscard. I'm going to try it out and if it doesn't work in six months, I'll leave. *That tells me right away that I would never sign that person.*
Harry Packwood
Harry Packwood Talent

What these quotes illustrate (regardless of the agent's point of view) is that the actor is questioning his own judgment. If you don't get in a position where you trust yourself and your instincts, how can you expect someone to hire you? How can you expect someone to put all his money and hard work on your judgments as an actor when you don't believe in yourself as a person?

Agent, Alan Willig put it very well: *Know thyself and trust your agent.*

Research

✓ peruse this book
✓ check SAG Agent/Client Lists
✓ study *The Academy Players Directory* and
  The Players Guide
✓ consult casting directors
✓ don't underestimate word of mouth
✓ have face-to-face meetings

Tools to Set Up Meetings

✓ referrals
✓ good credits
✓ awards
✓ beauty
✓ audition tapes
✓ a well written note stating your credits
✓ picture and credible resume

The Meeting

✓ be punctual
✓ act intelligently
✓ be sure to dress well
✓ be focused
✓ know what you want
✓ ask for what you want
✓ end the meeting
✓ set definite time for follow-up

7 Everybody's Responsibilities

Once you have made a decision, there are many things to do. If you are switching agents, it's only right to have a face to face meeting to say goodbye. Say you're sorry it didn't work out. Make it a point to speak to, and thank, all your agents as well as anyone else in the office for their efforts, pick up your pictures, tapes, etc. and leave. If the parting is amicable, buy your agent a drink if that's appropriate or you might want to send flowers. Send the necessary letters to the unions.

Setting Up Shop

The next stop is your new partner's office to sign contracts and meet and fix in your mind all the auxiliary people who will be working for you. If there are too many to remember on a first meeting, make notes as soon as you leave the office as to who is who and where they sit. Until you become more familiar with them, you can consult the map before subsequent visits.

Leave a supply of pictures, resumes and video-cassette tapes. Be sparing, for bringing supplies is always a good excuse for dropping by. Also leave a list of casting directors, producers and directors with whom you have relationships for *each* agent. Alphabetize them if you ever want them used. Also leave lists of your quotes (how much you were paid for your last jobs in theatre, film, and television) plus information about billing. The more background you give your agent, the better he can represent you.

Now the real work begins. Remember the agent only gets 10% of the money. You can't really expect him to do 100% of the work. That may be why you are leaving your old agent. You felt he didn't work hard enough. Maybe your expectations were out of line.

Maybe you were lazy. Maybe you didn't keep his enthusiasm high enough. Maybe he was a goof-off. Even if that was the case before, it really doesn't matter now. What matters now is how well you and your new agent are going to function together.

90%-10%

The concept of 90%-10% is fascinating. How many of us have resented our agents when we have been requested for a job and all the agent had to do was negotiate? In fact, if all our jobs were requests, would we just have a lawyer negotiate and do away with the agent altogether? Or is the support and feedback worth something?

Maybe our whole thought process about agents is incorrect. In our hearts, we really think the agent is going to get us a job. Based upon my years in the business and my research, I finally know that the agent does not get me work. He gets my appointments, but my work gets me work. Not only by my ability to function well as an actress, but also by my adjustment to life.

The times I have not worked as steadily have been directly connected to either physical or emotional growth spurts. I went into a terrible depression when my children left home. I willed myself to be up, but it was just a loss that I had to mourn. During that time, I was not particularly attractive to casting directors or anybody else. Life's processes must be endured. We can change agents and mates and clothes sizes, but we can't alter reality, we must experience it. Those realities are reflected in our work and ultimately enrich us as performers.

✦   *If you're not working because you are in your mid-life crisis, divorce, whatever, you may not be able to readily fix it, but it's up to you to assume you have a problem and set out to fix it.*
Martin Gage
The Gage Group

Although, we can hope that agents are going to initiate work for us and introduce us to the casting directors, producers, directors, etc., what they are really going to do over the span of a career is negotiate, initiate meetings, arrange appointments when we are requested and, hopefully, be supportive in our dark moments and help us retain our perspective in the bright ones. Notice I say moments. Neither state lasts as long as it seems.

Because we are getting 90% of the money (less taxes), we have to give up being cranky when we realize we are going to have to do 90% of the work. Since I assume you are willing to do that — if you only knew what that meant — let's talk about that.

What The Actor Can Do

✦   *The actor's job is to give me something I can go sell — a showcase, a new picture, a wonderful credit with a tour de force role. The second job is to be president of his own company — to treat the agent as his employee, to motivate him, to help guide the agent and to find a way to communicate with him so they can work as a team.*
Nancy Curtis
Harden-Curtis Associates

✦   *Actors are responsible for their own careers. Agents are just there as guidance points and buffer zones. If there is excitement about an actor, we can take it that much further, but the actor creates that excitement with his work and talent.*
Meg Mortimer

✦   *An actor is as much in control of his career and career choices as an agent, but an actor has to do his homework. You don't just sit back and say,* Oh, I've got an agent now. I can relax. *Look to see what plays are coming in on Broadway and off-Broadway. Stay on top of the scene. I know that sounds trendy, but it's your business. It needs that kind of energy.*
To be an actor is an extraordinarily difficult job and you've got to be working all the time on your craft, on your person.

That means your instrument better be tuned. At the same time that you're working on your acting, you've got to know what is going on. Knowing what is going on is half the job.

Mary Sames
Sames & Rollnick

✦ *The actor has to be very clear about what he wants and what he says. If he says he doesn't want to go out of town, but then misses out on an important project because it was out of town and gets mad at his agent, the agent is going to say* Well, you said you didn't want to go out of town. *Once you put qualifiers on your career, you are not going to have as many auditions.*

Ellie Goldberg
Kerin-Goldberg Associates

✦ *Actors have to give great auditions. They have to work really hard at what they do. They have to keep studying. They have to do research before they go into an audition. They have to ask questions of us. We get so busy in the office that sometimes I'll hear,* Well, you didn't tell me that. *Well, you didn't ask.*

The actor needs to take responsibility for asking questions. Don't expect us to spoon feed you everything. Actors have to be responsible for the basics of having an excellent picture, of making sure their reels are updated and of giving us information.

Meg Mortimer

✦ *An actor needs to be doing anything he can to establish a line of communication with people in the business who might provide him with information.*

Jerry Kahn
Jerry Kahn, Inc.

✦ *Keep your acting wheel greased by doing readings. This is very valuable. Everyone does them. You get to know a group of people.*

Charles Kerin
Kerin-Goldberg Associates

✦ *When an actor calls in and says,* Isn't that play *(whatever the name) coming in and aren't I right for that* part? *Well, it makes my job easier.*

Mary Sames
Sames & Rollnick

✦ *If I have to take time out from my day to talk to you to see how your day is going, then I'm not on the phone doing what I am supposed to be doing. If you hear of a project, make a two minute phone call,* I heard about this, is there anything in it for me? *That's the way to be a good partner.*

Ellie Goldberg
Kerin-Goldberg Associates

✦ *Actors have to go in there and really nail those auditions and meetings. Then, we can take the momentum they have created and create more momentum. I don't think an actor should expect an agent to do everything. It's up to the actor to get out there and make connections. He needs to be well-prepared and professional at his job so people want to work with him again. If he thinks that just because his last film was terrific that he is going to get the job, he's wrong. If he doesn't give the director and the producer what they are looking for, he's not going to get the job.*

Meg Mortimer

✦ *Make sure that we have enough pictures and up-to-date resumes without our having to call. If you are a musical comedy performer, be willing to go to an open call if we have discussed this is what you should do. It's important to keep working whether it's in a class or a workshop or a group; always keeping your instrument finely tuned. Networking is important, but don't expect that every time your friend gets an appointment that you will too, and just because you call or drop in all the time, that we are necessarily going to think of you more. You don't want to become a pest. It is a business, in spite of how casual it is.*

Gary Krasny
The Krasny Office

♦ *People at the beginning of their careers need to make as many connections as possible. I encourage communication. If they call me up and ask about a certain project, I want them to have done research so that they know if they are right for it.*

I have some clients and they hear about a movie and say get me in for this movie *and they don't even know if they are right for the movie. That's very annoying and then I don't listen to them anymore. It's like the boy who cried,* Wolf.

In New York, they can get involved in readings and can be readers for casting directors. I think it's a lot easier to network here than in Los Angeles, because of theatre and since people are out on the street, they run into people. You can say, I'd like to go to your reading. *That way you can get involved with another small group of people who are putting things together and those things build.*

Many actors define themselves as an actor and don't spend the time doing what they say they are and getting the training for who they say they are.

Meg Mortimer

Put yourself in the agent's position. Everyone in the world is trying to get his attention — the people who are already his clients and the people who are not. Only those people with sensitivity, creativity and smarts are going to make the appropriate impression.

♦ *Actors need to understand that up until 11:00 or 11:15 in the mornings, agents need to organize for the day, set up what Breakdowns they have to do, solve all the problems and handle the calls that came in at the end of the day before and they need to prepare calls that have to go out for the first part of the morning. This is organizational time for the agents.*

If the actor can just wait until 11:15 to call to find out about their next important piece of news, they would receive a more favorable response from the agent. Anytime after 11:15 and before 4:30 or 5:00.

Gary Krasny
The Krasny Office

✦   *Eighty percent of the scripts come from books and those books are yours to read. If you've read a book and you think the part of Joe Blow is right for you, I don't see why you don't go out and get hold of the people who have those rights and say,* Look, I read this book. I'm a fan of this writer.

Peter Beilin
Peter Beilin

✦   *Give me information I don't know about.*
Richard Astor
Richard Astor

✦   *I'm someone who encourages people to keep working. Not only on their craft, but just as a person. I think I've always been drawn to people who are, let's call them,* slightly neurotic about growth. *I'm a growth-oriented person. I like that people have interests other than just being insulated in the business, I guess that's because I think acting is about what you bring from your own life experience. You can see from the really great careers that they are people who have a lot going on. I do have a couple of clients once in a while that I have to get out of the rut of sitting and waiting for the phone to ring. Some of them have to get into a class situation. They'll feel better in class; scene study, audition classes, working with coaches. They need to keep moving.*

Peter Strain
Peter Strain & Associates/Los Angeles

✦   *Sometimes actors are under the assumption that the agent is going to get them the job. That's not within the agent's power. If it's between my client and another client, I can sometimes push it over the edge. Maybe I know the producer or the actor has worked for the director and I can call that director, but basically the actor is going to get the job ... or not. I can make the connections, but the actor gets the job.*

Meg Mortimer

✦   *Get seen. Do something to be seen because visibility is the name of the game. You're all competing for the attention of the casting director. You've got to do something to make them aware of your existence.*

Jerry Kahn
Jerry Kahn, Inc.

Classes are a good way to become part of the grapevine. When you get a day job, get one that has something to do with the business. Sell tickets at the theatre or be a waiter at Sardi's. You're creative, you'll think of something.

✦ *Be the best you can be at any given time. Study. Showcase your talent. Do showcases or little theatre. Make everyone you meet a human being.*

John Kimble
William Morris Agency

Important Details

✍ Have a pen and paper in your hand when you return your agent's call.

✍ Check in often.

✍ Return calls promptly.

✍ Make sure your agent never gets a busy signal; get call waiting.

✍ Take a picture and resume to every audition.

✍ Pay attention to common sense details of keeping lines of communication open.

✍ Trust your agent and follow his advice from picture and resume to what kinds of shows to audition for.

✍ Make sure your picture is in the current edition of *The Players Guide*.

✍ Provide your agent with ample supplies of pictures and resumes without being reminded.

✍ Go by and pick up the script before the audition.

✍ Arrive well prepared and on time at the audition (build in time for emergencies).

✍ Don't try to date the receptionist.

Networking

I know that networking is a dirty word to many of you. You say, *Oh, I'm not good at all that* or *I don't want to get a job just because I know someone* or *I'm here for art, not for commercialism* or some other elevated actor-jargon we all use from time to time to keep ourselves from testing our limits.

The most effective networking is done with your peers. You're not going to be able to pal around with Jerry Zaks or Christopher Durang. But, you can pal around with the *next* Jerry Zaks and the next Christopher Durang by becoming involved with playwriting groups.

If you make it your business to attend theatre whenever and wherever it's happening, you will begin to notice who the writers and directors are who are starting their careers. Focus on those whose work appeals to you. Go up to them and let them know you like their work. Give them your card and ask to be on their mailing list.

After you've seen their work a time or two, let them know that you are available if they need any kind of help. Become involved in their projects. You will all develop together.

It's hard to break in to what seems like the

charmed circle because people would rather work with people they already know and trust, particularly when a great deal of money is at stake. Wouldn't *you* rather work with friends and proven talent?

It is difficult behaving naturally around agents if you are not their peer, but if you are well read and cultivate an eye and ear for what's good, you'll be able to contribute to the conversation and begin to move toward the mainstream of the business.

Don't You Really Want To Work?

I'm a pretty quick study and, with concentration, I have the ability to memorize audition material and not hold the script for something as brief as a commercial. When I was a beginning actor, however, I would always hold the pages, because my background had taught me to be self-effacing, and it seemed to me that putting the sides down was too pushy; it would make them think I really wanted the job. On the day I decided to stop holding the script and take responsibility for the fact that I really did want the part, I began booking jobs.

I looked up *self-effacing* in the dictionary, it means *self-obliterating*. Don't *do* it. Sir Laurence Olivier used to ask anyone working on a project whether there was anything in it for him. If Lord Olivier could admit he wanted a job, am I going to pretend I don't?

Although I'm business-oriented about my career, I never thought about the 90%-10% aspect of things until I began researching my first book. I did think, when I finally signed with an agent in New York after successfully freelancing for a long time, that my own agenting efforts were over. From the perspective of time and research, I realize that because I was passive, I allowed opportunities to pass me by. That passivity kept me from educating myself and entering the system sooner in a more meaningful way.

Some actors become angry when they have to tell

their agents how to negotiate. They feel the agent is not doing his job if he has to be reminded to go for a particular kind of billing or per diem. We all need encouragement and respond to prodding. I don't like to admit it, but I can almost always do a better job if someone demands it. I might not think so initially, but scrutiny usually produces better results than my original effort.

If the agent does everything perfectly, great. But it's your career. It's up to you to know the union minimums and how to get your price up. It's up to you to figure out the billing you want and to help the agent get it. You are getting the 90%. Not only is it your responsibility, it's a way for you to be in control of your destiny in a business where it is too easy to feel tossed about by the whims of the gods.

Agents' Expectations

Before I talk about the Agents' Responsibilities, let's hear what agents expect from actors:

✦ *One of the things I expect from actors is that they love what they do. They may not love the getting the work part — but doing the work.*
Peter Beilin
Peter Beilin

✦ *If I sign an actor for a year, I expect (in that year) consistent callbacks. Or, let's say, I expect, at least, growth. I'm not going to look at somebody's track record and say,* You've been out on 50 things here and you haven't booked a job; I don't think there's anything we can do here. *It's difficult. It's very competitive. If I've believed in someone from the beginning, and if I see progress, if I see growth, and if I see the potential is still there, then I'm encouraged.*
Kenneth Kaplan
The Gersh Agency/Los Angeles

◆ *I don't expect the actor to get every job. Actors sometimes get embarrassed if they don't get the job. But once agents make a commitment to an actor, we're not talking three weeks or three months, we're talking, hopefully, about a long time.*

My commitment is for the long term because there's something in that actor that I respond to and you never know quite when it's going to break. I do have pretty much unlimited faith as long as we have communication. It's when the actor withdraws, when you don't have the communication you need, that you get into problems.

Pat House
Actors Group East

◆ *I expect that they'll prepare the audition material ahead of time, they'll show up punctually, that they won't be afraid to go out on a limb and take some risks with the material, that they will return my phone calls promptly.*

Gary Epstein
Epstein-Wyckoff & Associates

◆ *I expect my client to be on time, to be prepared, to be pleasant and to do the best job he can. Once I get you in the door, you are on your own. I think actors should not be afraid to take control of the situation. If they want to start over, they should say so. If they want to read different sides, they should ask for it. If they want to read another character, they should go for it. If they feel they were ignored, they should say so and not complain and whine to the agent.*

The actor is a grown-up and casting directors are not demi-gods, they are people even though they have total control. I don't mean the actor has to complain, but he should make it known that he wasn't comfortable.

Gary Krasny
The Krasny Office

◆ *Communication. Feedback. I want to know how the audition went the minute you leave there. Instantly. I need to know if it was sensational. I need to know if it was bad so that if I get a call from a casting director, that I know how to defend my client. I don't want to get a call from a casting director and have egg on my face.*

        Pat House
        Actors Group East

✦   *A client will say,* Are you angry with me because I didn't do so and so? No. *I'm giving you choices and opportunities. You make the decision and I'll go along with it. If I think it's a self-destructive point, I'll tell you. We can talk about it, but it's ultimately your decision.*

        Tim Angle
        Don Buchwald and Associates/Los Angeles

✦   *Don't suffer in silence. Don't do that. You short change yourself as well as me. I need to know a little bit of what is going on in the actor's mind. When I probe, I frequently find out that the actor is embarrassed that he hasn't gotten a job. I say,* Don't be silly; this isn't just for 10 minutes.

        Pat House
        Actors Group East

      The agent puts his reputation on the line by sending you in. And in every audition, you put your reputation on the line by the quality of your work:

✦   *My job is to get the appointment. Your job is to show up, sell yourself and do your thing.*

        Martin Gage
        The Gage Group

Agents' Responsibilities: What The Actor Has A Right To Expect

      All we want an agent to do for us is get us meetings for projects we are right for. This seemingly simple request requires of agents all the things that actors need to do; be informed and be professional, network, stay visible and communicate.

As we maintain our credibility by giving consistently good readings, the agent maintains his credibility every time we make a good showing. The agent has to build trust with the buyers so that when he calls and says, *See K Callan, you won't be sorry*, that the casting director knows he won't.

Then, if K Callan gets the job, the agent must be ready to do a wonderful job of negotiation, one that will make the actor (and the agent—he does get 10%) happy and at the same time make the casting director feel he got a bargain.

✦ *If the casting director gives me 20 minutes to submit people, I may call and say,* I don't need that much time, I only have two people. *I don't want to send people who are not right for it. I don't want to waste the casting director's or my client's time.*

Lionel Larner
Lionel Larner, Ltd.

The agent has all our responsibilities and more. The agent must maintain relationships with all of his clients and with the buyer. He must keep the buyers happy so that he can have return business. Although no buyer hires you because he likes your agent, if your agent can't get you in, the buyer will never get a chance to see how talented you are. Once in the buyer's presence, it's up to you to make your agent and the casting director look good by your brilliant work.

What The Actor Doesn't Have A Right To Expect

The actor/agent relationship is no different than any other relationship — no one likes to be presumed upon:

☺ *It is not okay to call your agent at home other than in an emergency.*

☹   *It is not okay to drop by the office unannounced and expect the agent to be available to talk to you.*

☹   *It is not okay to expect your agent to deal with your personal problems.*

☹   *It is not okay to arrive late (or very early) for meetings.*

☹   *It is not okay to expect to use the agent's phone for personal calls.*

☹   *It is not okay to hang around with the agent's staff when they are supposed to be working.*

☹   *It is not okay to bad-mouth the agent to others in the business. If you've got a gripe with the agent, take it up with him.*

☹   *It is not okay to interview new agents while your agent thinks your relationship is swell.*

☹   *It is not okay to call and say:* What's happening?

☹   *It is not okay to expect the agent to put all the energy into the relationship.*

Although many agents will be amenable to your dropping by, using the phone and visiting with the secretary, etc., it's best not to take these things for granted. After all, you want these people to be free to do business for you.

If you are not feeling confident about yourself, go to class, talk to a friend, a shrink, whatever, but don't burden your agent with that information. Will he feel like using up his credibility by calling casting directors and telling them that you are the best actor since Robert DeNiro when he knows you can't even get out of bed?

If you are not up to auditioning well, tell your

agent and postpone or cancel the audition. You are not only not going to be performing well enough to get the job, but people will also lose confidence in you and in your agent's instincts. It will be harder to get the buyer to see you next time.

Although the agent's main job is to get you appointments and negotiate, I believe you also have a right to expect him to consistently view your work and to consult with you before turning down offers. Your agents' advice regarding career moves is one of the things you are paying for. He is a conduit to and from the casting director and should convey feedback honestly about the impression you are making.

Make it clear you are ready to hear the bad with the good and you would prefer he express it in a con-structive manner. Not *You did lousy,* but *You were late* or *You were not prepared* or *The casting director said your energy was down.* Let him know that you want to remedy any problems, but that you need to know what they are. It's hard to assess auditions accurately without feedback.

Some agents give advice about pictures, resumes, dress, etc., but, unless you are just starting in the business or have just come to the New York City marketplace, established agents assume you have that all in tow and your relationship will suffer if they constantly feel you are asking for their time in matters that are basically your responsibility.

That said, you may ask if your agent is interested in having input regarding pictures. This is the agents' sales tool (along with an audition tape) and he may feel strongly that pictures are one area where he wants to take time to advise you. Sometimes I take my pictures to my agents for advice and sometimes I don't. My agents are busy and since they haven't made of point of asking me to consult them when I select new pictures, I frequently choose without their guidance and sometimes, they don't think I made the best choice.

If I were writing a book I thought agents would

read, I would suggest that periodically they call the actor in (whether the career is going well or not) and ask the actor to rate the agency. Is the actor feeling comfortable? Cared for? Serviced properly? An annual mutual rating wouldn't be a bad idea. Is the actor doing his part? Is feedback good? Pictures and/or resume need updating?

At contract renewal time, perhaps the agent himself (instead of an assistant) would call and say:

K, how are you? It's contract renewal time, I'd love to have you stop by and have a cup of coffee with me (lunch?) and have us talk about our relationship. We're still happy, we hope you are, but I'd like to get some input from you on what kind of job we're doing. Come in. We'll talk. We'll celebrate your contract renewal.

If I were suddenly a hot commodity, it would sure be a lot harder for me to think about leaving that agent for the attentions of ICM because I had been made to feel valued by the agent before my big break.

Staying In Touch

Keep in touch with your agent by being a good partner.

✦   *Call with information that will give the agent something to do:* I just got beautiful new pictures. I just did a mailing *or* I'm doing a show at EST. Can I come in and have five minutes to talk about a mailing about how to reach people? *or* Hey, I just heard at my commercial audition about this series that's casting. The actress who is going in and I are always up for the same role, I know I'm right for it. *Give me a tool I can use. Actors need to do 50% and I will do the other 50%.*
Nancy Curtis
Harden-Curtis Associates

✦   *Be seen visually by your agent on a regular basis.*
      John Kimble
      William Morris Agency

      Los Angeles manager, Ric Beddingfield says actors should make it a point to be seen by their agents once a week. Although most agents agree grudgingly that it is necessary for actors and their agents to be in constant contact, most agree that they hate to get a phone call that says, *What's going on?* They translate that into *Where's my appointment?* It's kind of like when you were little and your mom said, *What are you doing?* when she meant, *Is your home work done?*
      If you think about it from that perspective, perhaps you can find a way to have a conversation that does not make the agent feel defensive. If you are calling to say you've just gotten a good part in a showcase or just begun studying with a new teacher or, *Hey, did you see the new play at The Public? It's great, don't miss it,* the agent is going to be a lot happier to hear your voice or see your face.

✦   *I'm glad to have actors call in, but I do ask them to use discretion. Actors forget that every time I'm taking a call, that is less time I have to be agenting. If you are calling about a project, leave a message. They don't have to talk to me. The more time they leave me alone, the more time I have to agent. Please don't call and say,* What's going on? *That makes me crazier than anything else.*
      Mary Sames
      Sames & Rollnick

      It is true that if the agent is talking to you, he can't be talking about you. A Los Angeles agent put it succinctly: *My worst day is when I talk to more clients than buyers.*

Faxing

If you really really want to make a bad impression on an agent and guarantee that he will never be interested in you, fax him little notes, flyers and reminders of your existence. It may save you money and time to feed your flyer into his fax machine, but while you are doing that, you may well be disrupting his business. If he is expecting a contract or a deal memo and his line is busy because he is receiving a flyer from you, it's not going to make him kindly disposed in your direction.

A non-obnoxious way to stay in touch presents itself when you drop off pictures and resumes. Call ahead and say that you are going to drop off new pictures and want to pop in, say *hi* or ask the receptionist if you can just stick your head in once you get there. Late afternoon is best.

You can just be in the neighborhood and drop by to show a new wardrobe or haircut. Then be sure to do that; just poke your head in. Don't sit down unless asked and if asked, stay no more than five minutes. Be adorable and leave.

If you are depressed and need to really talk, call ahead and see if your agent has time for you. Suggest a cup of coffee after work or see if he has time for a snack in the middle of the afternoon — you can bring goodies. Everyone is happy to see a treat in the late afternoon. Since many folks are on diets, bring something healthy.

Make the effort to speak to everyone in the office and call them by their names. Get to know your agents and their support staff on a person-to-person basis. Learn something about each one of them so that you can establish personal relationships. You'll be able to say something that is not about you and/or the business. That will make all of you feel more comfortable.

✦   *The worst words are* calling to check in. *If you want to remind me of who you are, I always tell people to send me postcards.*

And send me a postcard that says something. Don't just send a postcard that says you are checking in. Tell me you got a job and are going off to do something or whatever. Don't tell me, Look I got this job; if you had sent me, you'd have gotten the commission.

Tell me you had a couple of callbacks for something or that you just got down to the wire on something, things that tell me about progress.

Flo Rothacker
DGRW

♦ *We don't need phone-ins. We don't have the manpower. We encourage people to let us know when they are in showcases. Obviously, we can't go to all of them. We usually end up picking reliable ones. By that, I mean reliable by reputation of the theatre, quality of production, the kind of cast they usually attract, and also the material. We stay away from showcases that do a lot of the classics. I don't think they're going to show the actor in anything we could sell them for.*

Peter Strain
Peter Strain & Associates/Los Angeles

It takes two energy-expending components to make any merger work. The agent must work hard for you all of the time and you need to deliver all of the time. If you don't stay abreast of what's in town, what shows are on television that might use your type, what you got paid for your last job, which casting directors you have met, who your fans are and, if you are late to appointments and ill-prepared, the agent is going to get cranky. If he doesn't drop you, he'll stop working for you. Worse, you'll get work anyway and he won't feel able to drop you; he'll just hate you.

If you are diligent and do everything you can do for your own career and consistently give your agent leads that he doesn't follow up on, then you're going to get cranky and leave.

It takes two.

Wrap Up

Details

✓ officially notify the previous agent that you are leaving

✓ take pictures, resumes, tapes, quotes, billing, etc., to new agents office

✓ meet everyone in the office

✓ make map of where everyone sits

90% — Actor's Part

✓ stay professionally informed

✓ network

✓ follow through

✓ communicate

✓ make informed suggestions

✓ get in a good acting class

✓ have call waiting/dependable answering machine or pager

✓ check in and return calls promptly

✓ stay visible

✓ be loyal

✓ pick up the sides

✓ be punctual

✓ do great auditions

✓ give and get feedback

10% — Agent's Part

✓ arrange meetings with casting directors, producers and directors

✓ arrange auditions

✓ negotiate

✓ network

✓ maintain credibility

✓ communicate

✓ make informed decisions
✓ stay professionally informed
✓ return phone calls promptly
✓ guide career

8 Self-Knowledge

Visionary, Buckminster Fuller said that if all the wealth of the world were redistributed equally, that in 25 to 50 years, there would be the same distribution of wealth we have today because not everyone would use the money wisely. According to Fuller, it's a law of physics.

That same law applies to actors. If all actors had the same talent and training, some would still be unemployed, because talent and training are the minimum requirements for survival. When people use the word talent, they usually refer to acting talent, but other talents govern how effective the acting talent can be. Efficient, stable, work-oriented actors will always win, over self-destructive, lazy actors who are chronically late and think the world owes them a living.

When you hear about the thousands of starving actors vying for five agents and one part, you can screen out many of those thousands. They won't be your competition because they have no appetite for taking care of business. It doesn't matter if there are only five agents and one part as long as you get the part and one of the agents.

I asked agents what was the most important single piece of advice they would like to give to actors who would read this book. Seventy-five percent of the New York agents said:

Know Which One You Are

Don't expect to play Sharon Stone's parts if you look like Joan Cusack. When I first arrived in New York, I did everything I could lest I be mistaken for the middle-class lady from Texas I was. I wanted to be a *New Yorker*. What I didn't realize, Texas accent not withstanding, was that my very middle-classness is what I have to sell. I have played women who went to Vassar, but more often, they can and will get someone who actually went to Vassar for those parts.

I'm an authentic lady from Texas who has raised three children and had various life experiences before, during and after. There is nobody else who has all my particular components. If I don't prize what is uniquely me and find a way to tie that to a universality of the life experience, not only will I not work consistently and honestly, but my life will be a mess as well.

✦ *I personally believe that anyone who comes into this business has one point where they can enter the business; a skill, a qualification that will get them a job tomorrow, literally.*

If they are willing to take the time to find out what it is and go for that area, they can get hired, they can start working. And then they can begin to explore the other areas they would like to do that they might not yet be prepared for.

There are certain qualifications that are required in every area. People who want to do musical theatre have to be able to sing and dance. They gotta take the classes. They've gotta do regional theatre and then work their way up, just like in corporate America. Those who want to do film and TV, other than those soap beauties who land a job just on their looks, you have to have certain qualifications.

Whatever area you are strongest in, you should go for that first. Then when you are making money in the business, you interview better and you audition better. You meet people better when you are working in the business than when you are a waiter or a waitress and trying to get just any job. You are going for film, you're going for commercials, you're going for television and just grabbing for everything rather than learning to focus and say, where can I get hired today?

Once you are working in the business, then you can move your way through the path you want to be on. That's the client I like to work with. One that is already at this point and we can

*move you from here to here to here and take you to where you want
to be. Then you are a goal oriented career driven type client.*

H. Shep Pamplin
Oppenheim-Christie

I asked Gary Krasny to list actor mistakes:

✦   *Not being in touch with who they are, what type they are,
their limitations, their strengths, their weaknesses, their inability to
grasp the fact that they can't be seen for everything in town and that
just because a friend gets an appointment doesn't mean he will get
one, too. They have to figure out what they are right for and what
they are best at; not knowing their own limitations.*

Gary Krasny
The Krasny Office

✦   *Many young actors are celebrity wanna-bes. They're not
process oriented. They're not working on their craft. They're not
working on who they are and what they do and making that the
best, bringing the life to it.*

*They're more goal oriented and looking just to get the job.
Unless you have the training, that one job you get is going to be a
flash in the pan. After that, that actor's career is over unless they
have a good solid foundation of training.*

Jim Flynn
Berman, Boals and Flynn, Inc.

✦   *A lot of people are just totally unrealistic. They're either
young and unattractive and/or overweight and inexperienced. And
they do have a chance of being an actor, but when you look like
that, it's not going to happen for 20 or 25 years. They'll have to be
a character person. They have a fantasy of acting and they haven't
done anything about it. They must do the work, they must learn the
craft.*

Lionel Larner
Lionel Larner Ltd.

✦   *Objectivity. An actor can develop objectivity. It's very difficult. I don't know how one does it, but one has to have a certain objectivity about oneself and not freak out in certain situations that are difficult; in a crisis, not to allow your emotional life to carry you over into decisions that are not correct decisions. Decisions have to be weighed over a period of time and not in hysteria.*

Jeff Hunter
William Morris Agency

✦   *Realistically, they've got to really look. If they want to be on a soap, they should know there are requirements to being on a soap. Training. Training and a certain look. Each soap has a different style and a different look. Someone says,* I want to be on a soap *and I say,* Which one? *and the actor doesn't know what they are or what soap hires what kind of person. Actors have to do their homework.*

William Schill
William Schill Agency

My friend struggled when she first came to Los Angeles. Today she is a big star. I remember the day I tried to help her by suggesting a part in a show I was doing. *Mary* was a pretty young actress with a broad range. The part I had mentioned to her was the town bad girl. She looked at me amazed and said, *K, you obviously don't see me for who I am. I have no breasts. No one will ever cast me in a part like that.*

She wasn't whining — just stating a fact. When she got her break, it was playing an upper crust young lady born with a silver spoon in her mouth. I'm sure the clarity with which she was able to see herself played a big role in her success.

✦   *Actors make a big mistake when they turn over their power to everybody else, making it about everybody else. Actors have to be very clear about who they are and what choices they are going to make when they go into auditions and if it's not working, to change their direction. You can't blame it on everybody else.*

Meg Mortimer

*◆   Actors don't understand how the business works. I can't
really blame them. All they want to do is act and everything seems
to get in the way of doing their piece. I feel bad about that.*

*They don't understand the reality of what it takes to get a
project on, the amount of money involved, the fact that everybody
involved is scared to death for their lives, their reputations, and that
when somebody comes walking through the door, they better be less
scared than these people are or they're not going to get the job.
Nobody's going to trust them with the money and the responsibilities
that go with some of the roles.*

Marvin Starkman/Producer

Sometimes we do get the idea that insecurity is
charming and that admitting it is even more endearing.
We announce to the buyers at an audition that we are
petrified of being there and that, because of this, we are
sure we won't do our best. Really? When *had* you planned
to do your best? In front of 5,000 people? Is that going
to be easier?

For the record, insecurity is not charming. It is
not appealing. And it is certainly not going to inspire the
people with money to trust you with the responsibility of
carrying their project. If you find yourself in a continuing
state of anxiety, there is either something wrong with you
physiologically or you are getting off on it. If you enjoy
being a basket case, take responsibility for that. This can
be a marketable attribute if you prepare yourself to play
those kinds of roles. Otherwise, get yourself together and
start behaving as though you have complete confidence
in your abilities. Pretty soon, you won't be pretending
anymore.

All we have is now. If you are not fulfilled by the
now, get out of the business. If the payoff for you is the
big bucks, the Tony or the Academy Award or the Emmy, change jobs now. You will miss your whole life waiting for the prize. If you are unlucky enough to get the
prize with this mind-set, you will find you are just the
same unhappy person, who now has an Academy Award,

that you were the day before.

Mental health, balance and self-esteem are necessities:

✦ *An actor is in a very tough position because he has to believe in himself in order to produce. On the other hand, there's a point where an actor believes so much in himself that he's unrealistic. There's a dichotomy between self-confidence and self-infatuation.*

Jeff Hunter
William Morris Agency

The late Barry Douglas from DGRW was articulate in his analysis of the actor's self-confidence:

✦ *The most important person to like you is the audience. Before the audience can like you, the producer has to agree to pay your salary. Before the producer agrees to pay your salary, the director has to agree to work with you.*

Before the director can agree to work with you, odds are, the casting director has to bring you in and say you're right for the role. Before the casting director can say you're right for the role, an agent has to submit you. Before any of these people get to see you, the first person who has to say, I'm good, *is the actor.*

You've got to be confident enough to take a risk with a piece of material, to look at a piece and say, Ah, I can expose the humanity of this character; I can develop the creativity of this moment of the theatre or film or television better than anyone in the universe. I am the first person on this. *If the actor doesn't believe that, no one else will. It's got to come from the actor first.*

✦ *Don't take it personally. If you don't get a job, that's not indicative of how good you were. There are so many things that come into play; age, size, coloring, if the voice quality didn't make the match they were looking for with other voice qualities and on and on and on. You could be the best at the job and still not get it. Some actors are crushed. They know they did a brilliant job.*

I hear from the casting director that the actor did a brilliant job and didn't get it. An actor has to have resiliency. It's a hard thing to have. He has to do a lot of work on himself personally. In order to be a good actor, you must keep yourself vulnerable and if you are vulnerable, you will take it personally.

You must get off it, go away from it, move on to the next thing. Be crushed and get on with it. Don't carry it with you. If you carry it to the next thing, you will be pulled under.

Bruce Levy
Bruce Levy Agency

And again, from Barry Douglas: *People who are too insecure to ask for an agent just might not make it.*

Reality

In a business of fantasy, the actor who makes it must maintain perspective and remain excruciatingly realistic about himself and the business.

✦ *Realize that everybody's career is different. Some one may be 25 years old and may be a star and then another actor may not make a dime until they are 50. Actors have to relax and not be so concerned with success.*

You have to be a constant actor. You can't say, Well, my friend is doing a Long Wharf show and I'm just doing Off-Broadway. *Everybody's career is different.*

Harry Packwood
Harry Packwood Talent

✦ *It's a business of survival. Your turn will come if you're good. It may not come as often as it should, but it'll come. They will eventually find you. You can make it if you can survive and you can only survive if you have no choice.*

If you go into the business saying, Well, I'll do this for five years and I'll see what it's like or I'll do something else, *if you have something else you can happily do, do it. It's only the people who are so committed, so desperate in some way that they'll put up with the humiliation, that they will allow themselves on ten minutes notice to be there, they'll allow themselves to be open and vulnerable, to still expose who they are and still be strong and closed enough to survive that kind of open wound life, they're the only ones who are going to make it, the people who have no choice.*

Barry Douglas

✦ *This is a business that rightfully or wrongfully, prefers prettier people. The prettier person gets the second look. It's a reflection of what the audience wants.*

Tim Angle
Don Buchwald & Associates/Los Angeles

✦ *I believe you will arrive at the success point you are intended to arrive at simply by working hard, not faltering and having confidence that it does happen. It does happen. You get where you're supposed to get in our business.*

Fifi Oscard
Fifi Oscard Agency, Inc.

✦ *Just because you don't get the job doesn't mean you're not good. There are many variables that you have no control over. An actor commits to a difficult life. He can't get a job and expect to be employed for five years like other people are. That is not an actor's life.*

Bruce Levy
Bruce Levy Agency

✦ *Don't look at other actors' careers from the wrong end of the telescope. Don't look at what they did and think,* Oh, they just went from one thing to the next. It was just this inevitable golden path and they just had to walk along it.

Tim Angle
Don Buchwald & Associates/Los Angeles

While you are paying your dues, you might get a job that gives you visibility and money for a month or even a year or two that makes you think you are further along in the process than you are. Once your series (only one job, after all, no matter how long it lasts) or movie or play is over, you are not visible in that show business way and you may think your career is over just because employment opportunities are no longer so high profile.

Visibility is a double-edged sword. In television, especially, the buyer may prefer a talented new face over an actor who has just finished a series. Frequently a semi-famous face finds itself unemployed because the buyer thinks it's too identifiable with a previous show.

Consistent Work

The task that takes more time than anything else is looking for and winning the work. Even two-time Academy Award winner, Sally Field says it isn't like she thought it would be. She's constantly reading scripts, looking for things. Then, when there is something wonderful to do, she still has lots of competitors.

That's depressing, isn't it? It never lets up. I think sometimes that if they just gave me all the jobs, that I might lose interest and leave the business. I certainly wouldn't mind putting that one to the test.

Assess Yourself & The Marketplace

Begin to actively assess which one you are. Are you a young character person? A juvenile? Someone who is right for a soap? In order to see yourself clearly within the framework of the business, study the marketplace. View theatre, television and film with distance. Notice what kinds of actors consistently work. What is common to the people that work? Notice who is like you and who is not. Keep a list of roles you have seen that you realistically think you would have been right for. Ask your agent if he agrees.

As you become informed about the business, you will begin to perceive the essence of people and notice its role in the casting process. More important than the look is essence. The thing that is the same in the many diverse roles of Robert De Niro is the strength of spirit.

Practice thinking like a casting director. Identify the essence of Alan Rickman, Billy Crystal and Whoopi Goldberg. Cast them in other people's roles. What would have been the effect if Tom Cruise had played John Travolta's part in *Pulp Fiction*? What if Julia Roberts had played Emma Thompson's part in *Sense and Sensibility*?

Impossible? Yes, but this exercise will help you understand why you will never be cast in certain roles and why no one else should be cast in your parts when you figure out what those parts are.

Does your appearance match your essence? Another responsibility you have is to be the best looking you that you can be, given what you came with. As Tim Angle said, *the business gravitates toward prettier people.* Just as in life. Getting upset about that fact is like throwing a fit because the sun shines in your window every morning and wakes you up. Get a shade. If you are not pretty, be clever.

There is an inspiring feature on the late Ruth Gordon in the *Los Angeles Times* that I reread in dark moments:

✦   *Two things first. Beauty and courage. These are the two most admired things in life. Beauty is Vivien Leigh, Garbo; you fall down in front of them. You don't have it? Get courage. It's what we're all in awe of. It's the New York Mets saying,* We'll make our own luck. *I got courage because I was five-foot-nothing and not showgirl-beautiful. Very few beauties are great actresses.*
     The Careerist Guide to Survival
     Paul Rosenfield
     The Los Angeles Times/Calendar Section
     April 25, 1982

The Process

✦ *Nobody changes the rules. What you can do is play the game for what you want or at least toward your ends. Nobody will force you to do work that you find insulting or demeaning. You have to figure out the rules in order to figure out how to play the game. You have to figure out what is a variable and what's not.*

If actors would take the time to put themselves in the shoes of the people they're dealing with, they would very quickly figure out what's reasonable and what's not. Actors don't understand why Equity Principal Auditions are a bad idea.

The reason is that no one can look at 250 people audition in a single day and give an accurate response. That's one of the reasons they only see 40 people for a role. Knowing that isn't going to make your life easier but it means it's not like some arbitrary system where God touches this person and says, You get to audition, *and you, as the untouched person, sit there wondering.*

If you think about a director casting a play and you understand what he has to do to cast it as well as possible, at least you know what you're up against. It's not some vague, amorphous obstacle. It's not fair but at least it makes sense.

What you know is never as bad as your imagination. If you know what you're up against, it can be difficult, but at least it's concrete. What you don't know, your imagination turns into, Everyone in the business knows I shouldn't be doing this. I'm just not talented. *It's like conspiracy theories.*

Tim Angle
Don Buchwald & Associates/Los Angeles

✦ *We'd all be a lot better off if actors knew what went on behind the agent's door — that it's actually a lot more simple and that there's not as much mystery about what happens between the agent and the casting director and the director and the producer as a lot of actors want to weave myths about. Most of the time, the actor is just not right for the part.*

Kenneth Kaplan
The Gersh Agency

◆   *Careers are like pyramids. You have to build a very solid
base. It takes a long time to do it and then you work your way up.
No single decision makes or breaks a career. I don't think actors
are ever in a position where it's the fork in the road or the road not
taken, where it's,* Now, okay, your career is now irrevocably
on this course. Too bad, you could have had that.

If an actor looks at another person's career and says, I
don't want that, *he doesn't have to have it. People do what they
want to do. It's like people who are on soaps for 20 years. Well, it's
a pretty darn good job, pays you a lot of money and if you're really
happy, great. But if you're an actor who doesn't want to do that,
you won't. Nobody makes you sign a contract. Again. And again.
And again.*

*Every decision you make is a risk because it's all collab-
orative and it can all stink. Every play at the Public is not a good
play. Every television series isn't a piece of junk. People make
decisions based on what price they want to pay, because there is a
price.*

*If you don't want to work in television, there's a price. If
you want to work in television, there's a price. If you want to work
in New York in theatre, there's a price. You have to decide if that's
worth it and it's an individual decision, not a moral choice. It
shouldn't be something you have to justify to anybody but yourself.*

*It's not about proving to your friends that you're an artist.
It's about what's important to you at that moment. People can do
two years on a soap and that can give them enough money to do five
years of theatre. And that's pretty important. It depends on why
you're doing it and what you're looking to get out of it, what is the
big picture. And nobody knows it but you.*

Tim Angle
Don Buchwald & Associates/Los Angeles

The second favorite piece of advice agents
wanted to impart to actors concerned marketing and
professional behavior.

◆   *I wish actors knew more about business things. It's hard.
When people have gone through school for four years or eight years*

and have gone through wonderful conservatory training, very seldom is any attention paid to the business aspect. People who have been working four to six years on their craft are suddenly here in New York where it's 50% craft and 50% business and they're not prepared and not knowledgeable about those situations. Simple things like pictures, resumes, answering machines, services, finding out about things they're right for. It's all business things.

Flo Rothacker
DGRW

◆   *One of the things I wish actors knew about was the business part of the business. A little bit more about their union rules and regulations so that every time you get an actor a job you don't have to explain to them what the contract entails. That information is as readily available to them as it is to the agent. It's irritating to have to go through all that when you book somebody.*

Jerry Kahn
Jerry Kahn, Inc.

◆   *Get a good picture that accurately represents you at your best. There are some photographers that take the most gorgeous pictures in the world and they don't look a damn thing like what the kids look like. You really want an accurate representation of who you are. It better be a look that you can duplicate when you walk into an office.*

Flo Rothacker
DGRW

◆   *Get seen. Do something to be seen. Visibility is the name of the game. You're competing for the attention of the casting people. You've got to do something to make them aware of your existence.*

Jerry Kahn
Jerry Kahn, Inc.

◆   *For the actor who wants to work all his life, the most important thing is continuity of management. Once you have established a reputation within the business that you are a good performer, the telephone generally rings. Your name is on a submission list.*

Yes, she's right for this. No, she's not right for that.
>   Jerry Hogan
>   *Henderson/Hogan*

Being Smart

The world is very small. The world of show business is even smaller; be circumspect with your comments about other people's work, about auditions, about casting directors and agents. You don't know who is listening or who is related to whom. Bonni Allen, who has now moved her office to Los Angeles underscores this truth:

✦   *Actors have to learn to keep their mouths shut except during auditions. Never talk in elevators. Never talk in rooms where you don't know people. Never. The bottom line is,* Don't talk.
>   Bonni Allen
>   *Bonni Allen*

I found Beverly Anderson to be one of the most candid, entertaining and helpful agents in town. When I asked her for her best advice, she thought for a moment and said:

✦   *Be smart. Don't be naive. If you're not smart, it doesn't make any difference how much talent you have or how beautiful you are. You're dead. In all my experience of 29 years, of all the people that I can sit here and say,* They made it, *they did not make it because they were the most talented or the most beautiful or even the best organized or the most driven. They made it because they were basically extremely smart human beings.*
*   It has nothing to do with the best looks and the best talents, the best voice or the best tap-dancing ability. It's being smart. Donna Mills is smart. Alan Alda is smart. Johnny Carson is smart. Barbara Walters is smart. They made it because they're smart, not because of talent. Talent is just automatic in this*

business.

Who's to say that Barbra Streisand has the best voice in the world? I mean, let's face it, she sings well and has gorgeous styling and she makes a great sound, but who's to say if she has the best voice?

I think the one ingredient that counts the most in this business is smarts. *You could be talented and be sucked in by some agent who signs you up and never sends you out and you sit there for five years and say,* Well, I thought they were going to get me a job. *Is that smart?* They promised they'd do a movie for me next year.

To be smart is the best thing. Talent is like a dime a dozen out the window.

Beverly Anderson
Beverly Anderson

Part of being smart is factoring in what your dream may cost. An interview with David Duchovny, star of *The X Files,* underscored information I have witnessed first hand:

✦   *I'm OK, I can take care of myself. But I feel isolated and lonely. I'm not happy. If I knew what it was going to be like, would I have taken the series? Can I also know what it would have been like if I didn't take the series? I hate those kinds of things, where people say,* Stop bitching, you could be working at Burger King now. *As if those are the only two options for me — either act, or* Would you like a soda with your fries? *But doing a television show is like riding an elephant — it goes where it wants, with or without your say. Does that make me an ungrateful bastard?*

Hiding in Plain Sight
Martha Frankel
Movieline
May 1997

We're back to Buckminster Fuller. Them that has, gets; them that don't, won't. It's all up to you and

Wrap Up

Analyze

✓   how the business works
✓   who gets hired
✓   who hires and why
✓   which actor is getting your parts?
✓   what do they have that you don't have?
✓   your strengths
✓   your weaknesses

Important

✓   focus on the process not the goal
✓   study
✓   nourish your talent
✓   be organized
✓   acquire business skills
✓   be smart

9 Star/Conglomerate Agencies

I guess we've all heard the joke about the actor who killed four people, ran over a baby, bombed a building, ran across the street into the William Morris Agency, and was never seen again. It's the quintessential actor story about the wisdom of being signed by a big conglomerate agency.

It certainly *seems* like it would be nice to have the same agent as Brad Pitt, Emma Thompson and Cameron Diaz. But, is it really a good choice for *you*?

The question is perplexing and research doesn't support a definitive answer. As in all other important decisions — who to marry, which doctor, lawyer, whether or not to have elective surgery, etc., your decision must be based upon a combination of investigation and instinct.

Research does lead to the conclusion that the star agencies — ICM, William Morris, CAA, United Talent — all have more information and the best likelihood of getting you in for meetings, auditions, and ultimately jobs, *if they want to.*

A successful writer friend of mine told of her adventure at one of the large conglomerates. She was making about $150,000 a year and an employer owed her money. She kept calling her agent asking him to pursue it. The agent was becoming increasingly irritated with her calls. She finally left when the agent said, *I really wish you were more successful and made more money so I wouldn't have to keep having these conversations with you.*

If $150,000 per year is not enough to get the attention of the big guys, there are a lot of other agents who will take your calls and treat you respectfully for a lot less.

What Do Casting Directors Think About Star Agencies?

I asked one casting director, *Who do you call first and why?* and he answered, *CAA, ICM, William Morris* and mentioned the name of a one-man office. The casting director said that although he can cast all the interesting parts from the conglomerates, he dare not skip this particular office because everyone on the list was special and capable of brilliance.

He explained that although many prestigious independent agents have hot new actors, the process is like shopping for a suit. If you want the best suit, you go to Bergdorf Goodman first. At Bloomingdale's, you can also get a beautiful suit and expect to spend a comparable amount of money, but Bergdorf not only has a suit, it has cachet — the perception that it is the source for the new and the unusual.

Casting directors tell me they prefer to deal with Elin Flack (Duva-Flak) and Phil Adelman (The Gage Group) and other distinguished independent agents and that an actor would be crazy to leave such prestigious independent agencies for a conglomerate. At the same time, since William Morris and ICM have made it their business to represent all the creative elements of the business, casting executives and producers acknowledge that if they want to do business with star actors, writers and directors, they will have to deal with the star agents.

It makes sense to choose an agency with a powerful client list, information and stature, however when I met a well-known actress at a party, she had other thoughts. The actress works mostly in film, but had recently been doing more theatre — an activity not prized by most conglomerate agencies since relatively little money is involved. She was unhappy that none of her agents bothered to view her performance: *It's too much trouble to keep up with all those agents. They won't all come see your work. Who needs it?*

I asked if she would return to the conglomerate if

she got hot and her answer was illuminating: *I was hot when I was at the smaller agency. My name was on everybody's list, anyway. I didn't need to have a big office behind me. The only way I'd ever go back to a big agency is with a very strong manager. That way, the manager could call and keep up with all those agents. So, no, I don't think it's necessarily a better business decision to be at a large conglomerate.*

It's true that the conglomerates have more power and information, but do power and information compensate for lack of personal attention? The strength of the large agencies comes from having a list of powerful stars and those bankable stars get the attention of the buyers and the agents.

✦ *Those who control the scripts, the actors — the information — rule the world.*
  Is This the Next Mike Ovitz?
  Joanna Schneller
  GQ
  May 1992

When you have John Travolta, Ashley Judd and Joe Eszterhas on your list, you have the attention of the buyers. The kicker is that if you are John or Ashley, you don't need star agencies — because you are the power — and if you are not John or Ashley, you are filler.

A big star was in the final stages of closing a deal on an big new movie, when a higher priced star at the same agency decided *he* was interested in the project. The original plans were shelved and the bigger paycheck did the movie. An independent agent might do the same thing, but the chances are less likely that he will be representing you and your closest competitor.

Packaging

A large agency representing writers, directors, producers and actors, has a script written by one of its writers with a great part for one of its stars or first-billed actors. It then selects one of its directors and/or producers and calls ABC (or Paramount or whomever) and says, *our star writer has just written a terrific script for our star actress and our star director is interested. Are you?* ABC says, *Yes*, and a package is sold.

Television pilots, TV movies and theatrical films are merchandised in this way. This phenomenon is called packaging. Non-star actors frequently choose agencies with package potential because they feel they, too, will get jobs out of the arrangement.

Daily Variety reported on the last detailed study regarding packaging in 1985. The statistics are still valid:

◆   *The SAG report released yesterday, flies in the face of traditional Hollywood lore, which has long held that an agency putting together a packaged project will utilize as many as possible of the performers it represents.*

The widespread belief that powerful agents routinely blackmail the studios into using their lesser known clients under threat of withholding their stars is a popular rumor with no basis in fact.

> *SAG Study Unwraps Package Myth*
> David Robb
> *Daily Variety*
> April 25, 1985

The study reviewed seven TV series, three mini-series and two feature films. It found of the 372 roles created for these packaged projects, only 27 went to actors who were represented by agents doing the packaging or slightly more than two roles per project.

◆   *You maybe can put the first-billed actor, maybe the second actor, but at that point people at the studios and the networks want their creative input.*

> John Kimble
> *William Morris Agency*

No Commissions On Packaging

If your agency packages a project in which you are cast, your agent is not allowed to charge commission because he is already getting a fee from the production company for packaging. This can be a good deal since you won't have to pay commission, but it offers no encouragement for your agent to place you in the package. He cares much more about the packaging fee and doesn't care much who is cast in it. Also, if you are tied up in a job for which the agent is not collecting commission, he is unable to sell you for something that he can make money on.

There are many horror stories recounting star clients who were never told of an offer of employment because the agents were withholding the star's services in order to get a packaging fee for the project. If the producers wouldn't go for it, the actor or writer or director never knew there had been an offer.

The value of packaging lies more importantly in the amount of access your agent is able to have with the buyers. Because the agent or someone at his company is talking to the buyers daily, there's naturally more of a feeling of comradeship.

Money Money Money Money

To some big agencies, it's all about money. It has to be. They have a big overhead. James Woods switched to ICM from CAA after a harrowing two years detailed in *Movieline*.

◆   *Sighing deeply, he observes,* If there was anybody meant to star in a Tarantino movie, it's me. Ten days after I went with Toni Howard and Ed Limato at ICM, they sent me up to meet Tarantino. The first words out of his mouth were, *Finally, I get to meet James Woods.* I'm sitting there thinking, *I haven't worked on a decent movie in two years and he's saying this? I said,* What do you mean? *and he said,* I wrote Mr. So-and-So in *Reservoir Dogs* for you. *I don't want to say the exact role because the actor who played the role is really wonderful.*

I said, Look, I've had a real bad year, so could you explain why you didn't offer it to me if you wrote it for me? *He said, We made a cash offer five times.* Of course, it was for less an amount than my [former] agents would want me to work for, but that's not the point. I wanted to cry. I'd rather work for a third of my salary and make *Reservoir Dogs.*

But I didn't get to do *Reservoir Dogs,* didn't get to know Quentin, so I didn't get to do *True Romance* or *Pulp Fiction.* All because somebody else decided money was more important. They were treating me like I was an idiot ... I made less money this year doing six movies than I made when I was at CAA doing two movies. And I couldn't be happier.

> *Out of the Woods*
> Stephen Rebello
> *Movieline*
> November 1994

So all conglomerates are not alike. If you are going to exist at this level, be sure to do your homework. Ask friends, stay aware of what is going on.

✦   *The problem is that they're too big and they can't possibly function as effectively for an individual client as any number of not huge agencies. I don't see it, even for a star. I don't see the personal attention. To me, negotiation is easy. You keep saying* no *until you get what you want.*

> Kenneth Kaplan
> *The Gersh Agency*

Kenneth gave me that quote when he was still an independent agent in New York. Since then, he has moved to The Gersh Agency, a bi-coastal agency with an important list of actors, writers, directors and below-the-line personnel. What does he say now?

♦ *Yeah. I know I said some things about conglomerate agencies in your last book. But, I have to admit that being able to work from the script instead of The Breakdown — which is really somebody else's interpretation of what the script is plus access to directors and producers — really does take a lot of frustration out of being an agent.*
Kenneth Kaplan
The Gersh Agency

♦ *I can give as fine a representation as the biggest agency in town if I'm enthusiastic about someone because it means I'm on the phone calling casting people, and they respond to my enthusiasm.*
Mary Sames
Sames & Rollnick

There are many prestigious independent agencies that have had a shot at the big time and chose to go back to a more intimate way of doing business.

One of my favorite agents has groomed several stars. When those actors became more successful and demanding, the agent grew tired of being awakened at midnight to endlessly discuss the next career move. It was disappointing when the actors went to WMA or ICM, but the agent just didn't see himself as a babysitter. Even Gene Parseghian (WMA) confessed that there are days when he wishes he still had a small office with three or four people and 20 clients, tops.

Sandy Bresler, a successful, distinguished Los Angeles agent (whose list includes Jack Nicholson, Judd Hirsch and Randy Quaid) left William Morris and started his own office. When that got too big for him, he left and started his own smaller office again. Of course, he did take Nicholson, Hirsch, et al. with him. That helped.

Conglomerates are not equipped to handle actors who are not making a lot of money. They are not interested in building careers. They take you while you're hot and they drop you when you're not.

A friend of mine was on a soap opera for ten years while her conglomerate agent collected his ten percent. When she was suddenly written out of the script, she went for an entire year without an audition before she wised up and left for an independent agency.

Get It While You're Young, You're Aging Even As You Read This

Star agencies are more interested in youth, not only because of the longevity factor, but because the most lucrative jobs in television and film (the leads) are for young, good-looking actors.

An actor usually needs the help of an independent agent or manager to catch the eye of one of the powerful agencies. Julia Roberts' career is a good example. She came to New York in 1985 with a famous older brother (Eric) already working in the business and hooked up with manager Bob McGowan.

◆   *To get Roberts a role in* Satisfaction, *a movie about an all-girl rock band, he lied:* Julia is a musician, *he informed the casting director — and enrolled her in a crash course in the drums, the easiest instrument to learn. Roberts got the part. When McGowan offered the prestigious William Morris Agency ten percent of the deal, it agreed to sign her up. Roberts was assigned to agent Risa Shapiro and Elaine Goldsmith in the company's West Coast office. They joined McGowan in guiding her career. The threesome lined up an episode of TV's* Crime Story *and a part in the HBO movie* Baja Oklahoma.
> The Power of Julia
> Elaine Dutka
> *The Los Angeles Times*
> June 9, 1991

Now Shapiro, Goldsmith and Roberts have moved to ICM and Julia has dumped McGowan.

✦   *... Roberts left McGowan, her manager, without explanation. She hasn't hired another.* That was the first completely difficult decision I had to make in my life, *she says.* Bob had gone to bat for me, but I felt I had to be honest. We'd outgrown each other. There were too many people around me making decisions and I wanted a clearer line between me and the work.

> *The Power of Julia*
> Elaine Dutka
> *Los Angeles Times*
> June 9, 1991

For insights into the motion picture business in all areas, particularly into life at the conglomerate agencies, I heartily recommend Mark Litwak's book, *Reel Power.*

Although all of us may dream a little of the validation we might feel would come with being a CAA client, as James Woods found out, sometimes that validation costs more than we might like to pay:

✦   *All CAA thinks about is the biggest salary you can get, period. My [former] agents were saying stuff like,* If you star in a movie with so-and-so, and it makes $100 million, then you can work with anybody. *I said,* You know what? I beg to differ. I don't think that if you do a movie with Pauly Shore, with all due respect, Sydney Pollack is then going to hire you.

> *Out of the Woods*
> Stephen Rebello
> *Movieline*
> November 1994

Among the Biggies, Who Is Best?

If fate leads you to the top, which diamond shines the brightest? According to *Daily Variety,* life in the stratosphere presents some interesting choices:

◆ *Not so very long ago, agenting in New York was defined by ICM's Sam Cohn...The landscape looks a lot different these days....The change is signaled by the resurgence of ICM and the William Morris Agency.*

WMA has been steadily rebuilding since the acquisition of Triad in late 1992. Particular strengths include the television department under Jim Griffin (including newscasting), theatre under George Lane, the lit department under Owen Laster and Robert Gottlieb, commercials under Brian Dubin in New York and a music and personal appearances group.

Agents Go Gotham
Diane Goldner
Daily Variety
August 29, 1997

◆ *Three agencies dominate the movie business: Creative Artists, International Creative Management and William Morris. The smaller United Talent also has a strong client list that includes stars (Jim Carrey and Sandra Bullock) and some top television actors and writer producers. A fifth agency, Endeavor, is also emerging as a power.*

Your Last Film Bombed? Simple: Get a New Agent
Bernard Weinraub
The New York Times
May 10, 1997

You'd probably be thrilled to be in the company of the names on the list of any large conglomerate agency. The casting people do say they call them first, mainly because the casting director is looking for a star to front a project.

But Robert Lantz, Lionel Larner, Martin Gage, Bret Adams, J. Michael Bloom, and other independent agents also have star clients and the access that goes with big name clients.

When all is said and done, the swell offices, script libraries, limos, flowers, and packaging considered, you'll make your decision based on what is important to you.

Do you want a family member or do you want a corporation?

My vote would be for the prestigious, tasteful mid-level agency. Of course, no one has plied me with limos and flowers yet either.

Wrap Up

Conglomerates

✓   have more information
✓   command more power
✓   have access to more perks
✓   can package effectively
✓   give less personal attention
✓   advice is corporate
✓   lose interest when you are not in demand
✓   have a big rent; need big revenue

Distinguished, Smaller Agencies Offer Possibilities of

✓   more respect
✓   more personal attention
✓   more empathy
✓   more freedom to experiment
✓   freedom for career fluctuations
✓   no limos
✓   no flowers
✓   no candy
✓   probably less information
✓   probably less access

10 Divorce

It's difficult to decide where to place information about relationships that don't work out. When I first started writing about agents, I began the book talking about this painful subject and vigilant folk pointed out that you have to have an agent before you can leave them.

That is true, but some people reading this book may already have an agent and are contemplating leaving. Even if you've never had an agent, you might find a discussion of relationship difficulties enlightening. The actor may be leaving just because he's not working and that may not be the agent's fault.

If your agent won't return your calls, if he's been dishonest or is not getting you out, those are legitimate reasons for leaving,

Maybe you and your agent have different ideas regarding your potential. This is something that should have been ironed out before the contract was signed, but when that conversation comes later in the relationship, reality must be faced.

Sometimes careers change and actors feel they can be better serviced by agents with a different set of contacts.

Perhaps your level of achievement in the business has risen. You have now, through brilliance or possibly a lucky break, become an actor of greater stature than your agent. (Very possible if fortune has just smiled on you.)

The bottom line is that actor/agent relationships are just like any other relationship: as long as it's mutually rewarding, everyone is happy, when it's not, things must change.

Actors and agents seek each other for mutual gain. The agent must see money-making potential to be interested in taking on partial responsibility for your career. 35 perfectly credible agents may pass on you and then agent number 36 will fall in love, send you to the right place with the right material and the right director, and you are suddenly a star.

It can happen the other way, too, of course. One minute you're hot and the next moment you're not. You didn't necessarily do anything so differently to get un-hot (frequently getting hot works the same way).

◆ *Jumping ship every six months (which a lot of actors do) only serves to hurt the actor because everybody knows about it and it shows that the actor can't necessarily get a job because something's wrong and it's not because of the agent.*
Gary Krasny
The Krasny Office

Before you replace and/or badmouth your agent, consider the following possibilities:

❖ You might have gained or lost weight and now no one knows what to do with you.

❖ You may be traveling into a new age category and have not yet finished the journey.

❖ You might be getting stale and need to study.

❖ You might be having personal problems that are reflected in your work; after all it's the life energy that fuels our talent and craft.

❖ The business might have changed, beautiful people may be in (or out).

How many projects can you list that had parts for you on which you were not seen? And were there really parts for you? You have to be right for a part not only physically and temperamentally but you must usually have the credits to support being seen for significant parts.

♦   *Actors don't do their homework. What part would you have been sent up for on a Broadway show? Yes, it would have been nice if you instead of Brad Pitt played the part in that film, but no agent would have sent you up for the part.*
Bret Adams
Bret Adams

Maybe the reason you want to change agents is that your friend seems to be getting more auditions than you. It is hard to listen to others speak of their good fortune when you are home contemplating suicide, but before you get out the razor blades, consider:

❖   Although you may frequently be seen for the same roles as your friend, there are aspects of your persona that are not the same.

❖   It cuts both ways. There have surely been roles that you were right for and your friend was not.

❖   You and your friend may be on different career levels.

❖   Perhaps your friend has not been totally candid in the descriptions of his auditions.

❖   It just may just not be your turn right now. Be patient, it will be.

Measure your progress against your own development. Your relationship with your agent should be judged on whether or not it is mutually rewarding and respectful. If your agent has been dishonest with you or if there have been financial improprieties, those are valid reasons to leave.
There are other kinds of dishonesty. I know an

actor who left his agent because the agent frequently told the actor how hard he had worked to get the actor in on projects for which the actor later found he had been requested.

Is Your Agent Doing His Part?

How can you tell if it's just not your turn or if the agent is not tending to your business? You can check with casting director friends, writers, directors and anyone else you know in the business. If you are being as involved as you should be, you'll be abreast of current projects so that you will have a realistic idea concerning projects for someone like you. Ask your agent for advice regarding what you can do to increase the number of your auditions. Discuss casting directors you would like to meet. Have a list of two or three who cast material you are career and type appropriate for.

Check with friends you trust to see if they have had any activity. Let them know you are not fishing for information, but just checking on your own paranoia: *Is my agent just not sending me out right now or is nothing going on?*

Drop by your agent's office with new pictures. Is the phone ringing? Are they are calling others? Or is the place calm with inactivity? If the office isn't busy, this may give you and your agent a chance to chat.

Communication

If you and your agent can't talk, that is a serious problem.

✦	*The biggest problem in the actor/agent relationship is lack of communication.*
Martin Gage
The Gage Group

✦	*If the actor had a meeting or is working with his agent and it's still not happening, I think the actor needs to leave. Even if he is afraid to. He can make a mistake the other way too, of course. If his career is going well, sometimes the actor changes agencies and he shouldn't, just because someone else is saying,* I can do this *and* I can do that. *Maybe he can't. That can be a mistake, too. You have to take an objective look at the situation.*

Meg Mortimer

✦ *Most of the time, when someone leaves, it's mutual. The bottom line is that it is the actor's career. If he is not happy, then it's up to him to say,* Can I have a meeting because it's been too long? *And then we will say,* What have you seen that you weren't up for? *Or* what have you heard of?

He might mention a project that he wasn't in on and we'll pull it out and see that on that project, they were looking for stars or younger or whatever. As soon as we talk about it, the problem is usually over. It's important, though, to have the conversation.

Ellie Goldberg
Kerin-Goldberg Associates

✦ *If the agent screws up a job, I think you should leave. If you don't get any appointments and you think you should be getting appointments, then you should move on to someone who is excited. If the agent doesn't take your phone calls, that's really a sign that there is something wrong. Sometimes you just have to get a fresh outlook. It works both ways.*

Gary Krasny
The Krasny Office

Bret Adams agrees:

✦ *I've heard actors say,* I haven't spoken to my agent in three months! *I've never heard an actor say,* I tried to get my agent on the phone for three months and I can't get through to him.

Bret Adams
Bret Adams

If you are not getting auditions, that may make you unhappy enough to change, but make sure you are being realistic. If there is nothing that's right for you right now—there's no getting around that.

Not everyone gets to do everything. Agents tell me the number one reason that a working actor leaves one prestigious, credible agent for another is that the actor sees his career in a different venue. If he's on soaps, he wants to be on primetime. If he's a television star, he wants to do films. When an actor becomes a star in one area of the business, that means (among other things) that many people are constantly telling the actor how terrific he is and how he can do anything. That may not be true.

Research your peers. Have they made that change? Some people have enormous breaks come their way, but not everybody is going to make a movie and not every actor is going to do Broadway.

✦   *I think you know what you've been submitted for; how many appointments you've gotten. You have to take the explanation of the agent and weigh it.*
Jeff Hunter
William Morris Agency

✦   *Every agent has different contacts. I may have fabulous theatre contacts and absolutely no film contacts. I might bullshit and tell the actor I have film contacts, but if you were that actor and I didn't get you a film audition for a year, you'd be getting the sense that what I was telling you is not true.*
Beverly Anderson
Beverly Anderson

✦   *We have to tell actors what we think they can realistically expect. That pierces their dreams sometimes and they move on.*
Jeff Hunter
William Morris Agency

The larger agencies are not in the business to handle less profitable jobs, so they either drop you or their lack of interest finally tells you that you're no longer on their level. This is the moment when you might be sorry you left that swell agent who worked so hard to get you started and engineered the big break for you. Will he want to see you now? He might. He might not. It depends on how you handled it when you left.

Maybe your career is doing okay but you feel you haven't progressed in several years.

Some actors leave their agents on a manager's advice. Sometimes that's a good idea, although it's possible the manager is just jealous of the relationship the actor has with his agent and wants to put himself in a more powerful position.

Maybe you want to leave your agent because the magic has gone out of your marriage just as the magic can go out of a traditional marriage if both partners don't put energy into it. Check the discussion of the actor's responsibilities in Chapter Seven for some ideas on how to infuse life into the partnership. If you are both willing to save the alliance, that will take a lot less energy and resourcefulness than going through the *just learning to get to know each other* period involved in any new relationship.

✦ *The bottom line is you're not getting work. It doesn't make any difference what the reason is. If you're not getting work, you have the right to leave and if you're smart, you will leave.*
Beverly Anderson
Beverly Anderson

Don't Wait Until It's Too Late

Just like anything else, if something is bothering you, speak up. Candor comes easily to very few people. We all want to be liked and it's not pleasant to confront people. If you are not going out, call your agent and tell him you are concerned. He knows as well as you that you are not going out. Ask him if there is anything you can do. Ask if he has heard any negative feedback. But, whatever you do, don't just start interviewing for a new agent and badmouthing your present agent. Although it's easier to whine to bystanders about your dissatisfaction instead of dealing with your agent, that's not only a childish thing to do, it's ineffective, dishonest and makes you look bad. If you intend to succeed in this business, you'll have to do better than that.

✦   *Early on, at some moment, discuss problems with the agent. There are actors who hide in their kitchens, angry because they have not had auditions. By the time they can't stand it any longer, they call and tell you they're leaving. We're not omniscient; we don't know sometimes what is happening or not happening.*

We have meetings every week at the office and discuss all the clients and we might know someone is dissatisfied. But even if we miss it, you are obliged to come in and speak to your agent, not an assistant, because you are signed by the agent. Then we'll discuss it. We'll have a discussion and try to solve it.
Fifi Oscard
Fifi Oscard Agency, Inc.

Leaving Your Agent

If you did wait too long and it's too late for a talk or if the talk didn't help, at least leave with a little class. Though it might be uncomfortable, get on with it:

✦   *I would be very upset if someone with whom I've had a long relationship fired me by letter. I think it would be the ultimate rudeness, ingratitude, lack of appreciation for the work I've done. Get past the guilt, the embarrassment. I'm owed a certain consideration. Deal with it. I understand the difficulty, but that's not an excuse.*
Phil Adelman
The Gage Group

So be a grownup — you owe your agent the courtesy of a personal meeting. Go in and talk to him. Explain that, for whatever reason, it's just not working. No need for long recriminations. No excuses. Not, *My wife thinks* or *My manager thinks*. Simply say, *I've decided that I am going to make a change. I appreciate all the work you have done for me. I will miss seeing you but it just seems like the time to make a change. I hope we'll see each other again.*

Write your own script, these words are just to spark your imagination. No need to be phony. If you don't appreciate what the guy has done and don't think he's done any work, just skip it. Talk about the fact that you think the relationship is not, or is no longer, mutually rewarding. Leave your disappointment and anger at home. Be straightforward and honest and you'll both be left with some dignity. You may see this person again and with some distance between you, you might even remember why you signed with him in the first place. Don't close doors.

If you are leaving because your fortunes have risen, the meeting will be even more difficult because the agent will really be upset to see you and your money leave. Also, your newfound success has probably come from his efforts as well as yours. But if you are really hot and feel only WMA, ICM or another star agency can handle you, then, leave you must.

Tell him you wish it were another way but the vicissitudes of the business indicate that at a certain career level, CAA and peers have more information, clout, and other stars to bargain with, and you want to go for it. If you handle it well and if he is smart, he will leave the door open. It has happened to him before and it will happen to him again. That doesn't make it hurt less, but this is business. He will probably just shake his head and tell his friends you have gone crazy and that: *This isn't the same Mary I always knew. Success has gone to her head.*

He has to find some way to handle the rejection just as you would if he were firing you. It will not be easy to begin a new business relationship, but you are hot right now and the world is rosy.

Wrap Up

Questionable Reasons for Leaving

✓ no recent work
✓ manager pressure
✓ agent disinterest

Better Remedies than Leaving Agent

✓ learn to communicate better with your agent
✓ take a class, study with a coach
✓ do a showcase
✓ court casting directors
✓ put your own project together

Clear-Cut Reasons for Leaving

✓ lack of respect
✓ dishonesty
✓ communication didn't help
✓ differing goals
✓ personality differences
✓ sudden career change for better *or* worse

Speak to Agent

✓ before things get bad
✓ before interviewing new agents

11 Managers/TOS/Etc.

My experiences with managers don't generally lead me to recommend them. Under any kind of normal circumstances, it seems odd to me that someone would want to spend a minimum of 15% of their income to get the service we all hope to get from our agent.

When It Makes Sense To Have A Manager

Managers are a definite plus for child actors who need guidance and whose families have no show business background. A manager usually places the child with an agent, monitors auditions and sometimes even accompanies the child to meetings and auditions.

If you are entering the business and need someone to help you with pictures, resumes, image, etc., managers can be helpful. There are, however, many agents who delight in starting new talent and consider this part of their service.

When you are at a big agency and it's too intimidating and time consuming to keep in touch with 20 agents, it might be advantageous to have a connected manager in your corner.

Changing agents is easier when you have a manager, because the manager does all the research, calling and rejecting of the former agent. If agent changing is the only reason you have engaged the services of a manager, it's an expensive antidote to one uncomfortable meeting.

If you have the credits to support getting a good agent, you can do that on your own. If you don't, the manager can't create them.

I have a few friends who feel the presence of a manager enhanced their careers — at least momentarily. One in particular said her agents were considering dropping her, so she and the manager decided to make her more attractive to the agents by getting some jobs themselves. They read The Breakdown and the actress delivered her own submissions to the casting offices.

If the manager got a call for an appointment, the actress went in and if she got the job, they called the agent to make the deal. The agent became more enthusiastic about the actress for a while, but ultimately dropped her. The agent's earlier disinterest signaled what he had already decided: that the actress was no longer appropriate for his list. In that case, the manager, though helpful, only delayed the inevitable.

No License Required

Although there are many important, effective and honest managers, there are many who are not. Agents must be franchised by the entertainment unions and the state, displaying at least a modicum of track record, honesty and skills before they are certified. There is no certifying group overseeing the activity or contracts of managers who can charge whatever they can get away with and they can tie you up for years. When Eddie Murphy became successful, an enterprising manager appeared from his past claiming part of the spoils. He had a valid contract. I don't know what Murphy ended up paying, but the aggravation and court costs were not inconsiderable. Be careful.

Top Of The Show/Major Role

A phrase heard more in Los Angeles than in New York, TOS/MR refers to wages paid to guests in television episodes. Years ago guest stars received $10,000 or more per week. In 1961, television reruns became subject to residual payments to actors. Production company managements got together and decided to stop negotiating with actors playing guest leads in episodes, setting a predetermined cap for appearances on half-hour and hour shows.

Screen Actors Guild minimum (principal work)

per day is $559 on a film or a television show, a very good fee. If you are fortunate enough to work for five consecutive days, however, instead of being paid $2,795 (which is five times the minimum) there is a discounted rate, $1,942. The discount results in a per day fee of $388.40 or less than scale for a day's work. The discount was agreed to by Screen Actors Guild to encourage the hiring of actors for more days of employment.

In the recent past, SAG has addressed the discount by adding the Top Of Show/Major Role designation as part of the contract, which actually just gets you back up to scale less the discount.

The TOS/MR designation is a guaranteed number of days predicated on guest star billing. The fee difference between half-hour and hour shows is the guarantee; half-hour now guarantees five days employment at $559 per day, an hour show guarantees seven days. Days over the guarantee are paid at the same scale rate per day: $559.

There's nothing wrong in working for minimum if that is where your rate is, but management, by attaching the Top of the Show/Major Role designation, throw the phrase around as though an actor is getting some kind of preferred rate. The only real money goes to high visibility actors who routinely command $15,000 for an appearance on an hour show.

There are a few shows, notably those produced by Aaron Spelling in Los Angeles, that routinely break the top or have no top, but they also routinely hire stars whose fees are far above TOS/MR. Stephen Spielberg also pays pretty well: the grapevine says Charlton Heston made $85,000 for an appearance on *Seaquest DSV*.

By and large, it has always been easier to negotiate for above-scale film and television money in Los Angeles than in New York. But even in LA, management has begun to cut supporting actors' wages in favor of the salaries of producers, writers and stars.

The Breakdown Service

Before The Breakdown Service existed, agents in Los Angeles had to drive to each studio every day, read each script, make their submissions and repeat the process at the next studio. Finally, an enterprising chap named Gary Marsh (who had to read all the scripts anyway for his mother, an agent) called the studios and said something like: *I think I could make your life better. If you give me all your scripts, I will summarize them and make a list of the types of actors needed for the parts, the size of each role, etc., and provide that information to all the agents. This will save you the nuisance of having all those people in your offices and them the inconvenience of driving.*

Thus, the much maligned Breakdown Service was born. It costs the agents a hefty amount, but it's worth it. When agents subscribe, they must agree not to show it to actors. As it is, casting directors are unable to deal with every agent in town, so there is no possibility that they would have time to sift through actors' submissions as well.

Some actors get their hands on The Breakdown, anyway. I knew of a woman in Beverly Hills who charged actors $20 per month for access to The Breakdown. She hid it under a rock behind a gate. Actors drove up, lifted the rock, sat in their cars, perused The Breakdown and made notes. Then, they returned it to its hiding place and drove away.

✦ *Getting The Breakdown is the worst thing an actor can do. A breakdown isn't just a black and white piece of paper. The casting director calls the information in the day before The Breakdown comes out. By the time it comes out, that role may have changed. If the actor is reading it, he doesn't know that. It's depressing. He can't understand why he isn't called for a role that doesn't even exist anymore.*
Mike Eisenstadt
Amsel, Eisenstadt & Frazier, Inc.

Whereas some actors are able to use the pur-loined information intelligently, others merely alienate their agents with it.

Although The Breakdown is invaluable, it doesn't include everything. Many episodic parts are filled by casting directors who just call and ask for the actors they want to see. Frequently this is because the script is truly not available. Also, many films do not come out in Breakdown unless the casting director needs an unusual actor for a role. Most of the time, they just call and ask for whomever they want.

Since not everything comes out in Breakdown, it is important to assess your agent's other contacts. If your agent is not in a position to have more information than is in The Breakdown, that's still a lot of information, if he uses it wisely.

The Breakdown is now not only part of the New York/Los Angeles casting scene, but it is available via the Internet.

Your Reference Library

When I was still living in New York, I was fortunate enough to get a part in what turned out to be an important film called *A Touch of Class* which shot in Spain. The night I arrived in Marbella, I found myself standing next to the wife of the writer-producer-director at a party honoring the cast. Making conversation and truly delighted to be involved with such a lovely script (Mel Frank eventually won an Oscar for it), I said to Ann Frank: *What a wonderful script. Is this Mel's first script?* What did I know? I thought he was primarily a director and as a New York actress, I was ignorant of things Hollywood.

Ann was so cool. She neither walked away nor behaved in any way condescending. She just began pat-iently enumerating the edited version of her husband's incomparable credits. It turned out that Mel was a famous Hollywood writer, and along with partner, Norman Panama had written the Bing Crosby-Bob Hope

Road pictures, plus many other classic films.

I almost died of embarrassment, but Mrs. Frank was all class. She patted my arm and smiled: *This will be our little secret.* All the time I was apologizing for my ignorance, I was promising myself that I would never be in that position again.

I now own many books that have the credits of writers, directors and producers and I strongly suggest you begin assembling a library of similar information. I also recommend your library be stocked with books that tell you what the business is really like (*Adventures in the Screen Trade, The Season,* and *Final Cut,* etc.), as well as biographies of successful people (in our business and others) that will provide role models in your quest for achievement.

Here is a list of books that will give your library a good start:

Aaron Spelling: a primetime life/Aaron Spelling
Adventures in the Screen Trade/William Goldman
AFTRA Agency Regulations
A Passion for Acting/Allan Miller
Audition/Michael Shurtleff
casting by ... A directory of the Casting Society of America,
    its members and their credits
The Complete Directory to Primetime Network TV
    Shows/Tim Brooks-Earle Marsh
The Devil's Candy/Julie Salamon
Equity Agency Regulations
The Film Encyclopedia/Ephraim Katz
The Filmgoer's Companion/Leslie Halliwell
Final Cut/Steven Bach
Halliwell's Film Guide/Leslie Halliwell
Hollywood Agents & Managers Directory/Hollywood
    Creative Directory
Hollywood Creative Directory/Hollywood Creative Directory
How I Made 100 Films in Hollywood and Never Lost a
    Dime/Roger Corman
How to Sell Yourself as an Actor/K Callan

Hype & Glory/William Goldman
Indecent Exposure/David McClintock
The Last Great Ride/Brandon Tartikoff
The Los Angeles Agent Book/K Callan
Making Movies/Sydney Lumet
My Lives/Roseanne
The New York Agent Book/K Callan
New York Times Directory of Film/Arno Press
New York Times Directory of Theatre/Arno Press
*Next: An Actor's Guide
       to Auditioning*/Ellie Kanter-Paul Bens
Ovitz/Robert Slater
Rebel Without a Crew/Robert Rodriquez
Reel Power/Mark Litwak
Ross Reports Television/Television Index
Saturday Night Live/Doug Hall-Jeff Weingrad
Screen Actors Guild Agency Regulations
Screen World/John Willis
The Season/William Goldman
Theatre World/John Willis
TV Movies/Leonard Maltin
You'll Never Eat Lunch in this Town Again/Julia Phillips
Wake Me When It's Funny/Garry Marshall
Who's Who in the Motion Picture Industry/Rodman Gregg
Who's Who in American Film Now/James Monaco
Wired/Bob Woodward

If you know of any books that belong on this list,
let me know and I'll include them in subsequent editions.

I consider books like *Wired*, *Indecent Exposure* and
Saturday Night Live to be instructive and realistic about the
business. I keep them on my bookshelf to keep my values
in perspective. I want to remember how easy it is to get
caught up in the glamour, publicity, money and power of
this fairytale business. I want to remember that those
things leave as quickly as they come. I need these books
to remind me why I got into the business in the first
place. I have to strive to remember that success doesn't
fix you. It may feel better for a while, but you're always

you — just with a different set of problems.

I cannot stress strongly enough the need for a good reference library.

For fun, read Tony Randall's book, *Which Reminds Me*; for inspiration, Carol Burnett's *One More Time*; and to hear about more bad luck than you'll ever have, read Charles Grodin's *It Would Be So Nice if You Weren't Here*. Roseanne's book, *My Lives,* speaks candidly of the behind-the-scenes intrigue involved with her show. It's instructive.

Wrap Up

Managers

✓ can provide access
✓ can provide guidance
✓ are expensive
✓ are not governed by industry standard contracts
— be careful

The Breakdown Service

✓ important tool for agents
✓ can be self-destructive in the hands of the wrong actor

Reference Library

✓ educational
✓ inspirational
✓ indispensable

12 Stand-Ups/Children

Abbott and Costello, Jack Benny, Chevy Chase, Roseanne, Whoopi Goldberg — the list of successful performers and stand-up comics who crossed over into films and television is impressive. Today, added to that list are performers who write, stage and act in their own one person shows. Theatrical agents don't deal with this type of performer per se, so in this edition, I interviewed a few agencies who specialize in this area of the business. The longer version of this information is in my book, *How to Sell Yourself as an Actor*, but I'll fill you in briefly on what these people expect.

✦ *We've definitely steered toward a very personality oriented comic. A charismatic style comic.* The Tonight Show *might use a comic because they're a very good comic in terms of their writing. A structural comic who writes a perfect setup and a punch line. Some of those comics wouldn't crossover into a sitcom because they might just be joke tellers. We want somebody who is a very full bodied character a la Roseanne, Tim Allen, Seinfeld. The development and casting people are looking for that. They are already walking in with a character. Some comics have stronger skills in that area.*
Bruce Smith
Omnipop

✦ *A lot of comedy clubs have closed across the country, but there are still a fair amount in the northeast so it's easier to keep a comic working there as they start to develop. The more stage time they get, they better they become. We encourage them to get into acting classes, not to become actors, but just to start. We want to know what their long range goals are. In order for a comic to become popular, he needs television exposure. If you can support that with a strong act, you're going to have a good career.*
Tom Ingegno
Omnipop

✦   *I wouldn't assume that just because you are a comedic actor that you can do stand-up. Soap opera people try to do stand-up. Most of them, because they are so pretty have not lived that angst ridden life that comics have. It becomes a frivolous version of comedy. The first thing you want to establish with an actor that is going into comedy is: Do they have a natural feel for it? Do they have comedic rhythm for it? There are many actors who are wonderful with comedy, but can't do stand-up. You need the stage time.*

>   Bruce Smith
>   *Omnipop*

✦   *A comedic person has to have the backing of the theatrical training, otherwise you're looking at a personality oriented project. Many stand-ups came out of theater and did stand-up as a means of survival.*

>   Steve Tellez
>   *CAA*

The personal appearance agents that I spoke to supported what I have learned from theatrical agents and scriptwriters' agents. None of them are interested in one shot representation.

If you get a guest shot on *Friends* and call an agent with that shot as an entree, he will probably take your call, but if you don't have a track record of credits (they don't all have to be as important as *Friends)* then the credible agent is not going to be interested. 10% of an episode is not enough for him to put you on his list to share all his introductions and hard work.

If you have written a one-person show and Disney is interested, that might be interesting to a stand-up agent, but probably not. Development deals go south with regularity and if you don't already have a stand-up career going for yourself, personal appearance agents are not going to be interested. They want people who have been playing clubs in and out of town and have the stage time.

Stand-up and performance artist shows are a bonafide way to be entrepreneurial about the business, but there are no short-cuts to theatrical/comedic maturity. You gotta do the time.

Children In The Business

Children and parents of children who want to be involved in show business: be advised that I don't think it is a good idea. You only get a shot at being a child and being taken care of once in your life. If you blow that, you are up a creek.

The tabloids make a lot of money running stories on the messed-up lives of former child actors. I know you think you and/or your children could never have those problems. Maybe you won't. Just think seriously about what you are getting into before you take the next steps. If your child is paying your rent, the balance of power tips and there is no more family hierarchy. Remember Macauley Culkin.

That said, if you are still interested. Here's the procedure. Professional experience is not necessary, but it helps.

Children's agents do not expect professional pictures, children change too quickly, it's a waste of money. Agents are perfectly happy to see snapshots of your child. Either mail them in with a note giving all the vital statistics — age, weight, height, coloring and anything the child might have done involving getting up in front of people and taking direction. What your child absolutely must be is comfortable with people. Happy. Confident. Gregarious.

If the picture interests the agent, he will ask you to bring the child in for an interview. The agent will expect to speak to the child alone. You will be invited out while the agent gets a feel for how the child is in the same kind of meeting situation that will take place with an audition.

If you are a child reading this, let me tell you that agents are very impressed when a child makes his or her own arrangements. It means you are motivated, organized and adult about the whole thing. A children's agent told me that her role model for a child actor was a client who at 13 had done lots of local theater, called Screen Actors Guild, got a list of agents and sent in pictures himself. He got a manager and the manager got him the agent. He got the first job he went for: the national tour of *The Sound of Music.*

Children are paid the same fee per day as adults and will be (all things being equal) expected to behave as an adult. No sulking, tantrums or crankiness. (They don't like it when adult actors do that either!)

Set Sitters

Parents should be prepared to ferry children to many auditions and if the child books a job, to be on the set with him at all times. Not only is it a SAG rule that a parent or designated set sitter of some type be provided, but it is unwise ever to leave your child in an adult environment on his own.

Someone needs to be there to be your child's advocate. No matter what the job or how good management is about things, they are in the business to make money. Someone must be there who is not afraid of losing his job if he speaks up that the set is too hot or the kid needs a break. We all want to please and do a good job, but certain rules must be followed.

You or your designated representative should be there. And you should have both read the Screen Actors Guild, Equity and AFTRA rules so that you know when the child must be in school or resting or has a right to a break. You should also know about overtime and payment for fittings. SAG has a book for young performers that's yours for the asking.

Many child actors work through managers. It's

not necessary, but managers can be helpful at this stage by putting a child together with an agent and making recommendations concerning dress, pictures, study and so on. Many parents fulfill the same role and many agents expect to provide the same service without an additional charge of 15%.

So saying, it's imperative that parents recognize their role in the process.

✦ What parents have to understand is, they are the excess baggage that comes along with the talent, *says Innovative Artists' Claudia Black.* It's the parent's responsibility to make sure the child is prepared, on time and has rehearsed the scene....*If agents can't get along with the parent, they won't take the kid.* It's really not just about the kid being amazing, *says Cunningham Escott Dipene's Alison Newman, It's a joint thing, fifty-fifty.*
Do, Re, Me Me Me!
Alexandra Lange
New York Magazine
November 10, 1997

Wrap Up

Standups

✓ need 15-20 minutes of material to begin
✓ need a persona
✓ should have theatrical training
✓ gotta do the stage time

Children

✓ a snapshot will do to begin with
✓ paid as an adult — must behave like one
✓ must be able to talk to anyone
✓ set-sitter required
✓ it's the parents' job too

13 Researching the Agents

There are various categories of agencies; big, small, conglomerate, beginning, the-next-big-thing and/or just getting by. Since agency/client relationships are so personal, any classifications I might make would only be subjective, so I'm presenting you the facts as best I can, based upon my research and personal experience both in interviewing these agents and my years in the business.

There are new agencies with terrific agents building their lists who, like you, will be the stars of tomorrow. You could become a star with the right one man/woman office and you could die on the vine at ICM. There are no guarantees, no matter whom you choose. The most important office in town might sign you even without a single credit if your look excites them. But mostly, they want you when you are further along. Whomever you choose, if you are to have a career of longevity, you can never surrender your own vigilance in the process of your own destiny.

If you read carefully, you will be able to make an intelligent decision using client lists, the agents' own words, and the listing of each agency. It's unwise to write off anybody. In this business, you just don't know. One's own tastes and needs color the picture. I could have an agent I love and you might hate him.

There are nice agents who are good agents and there are nice agents who are bad agents. There are agents who are not nice who are good agents and so on. Just because I may think some agent is a jerk doesn't mean he is. And even if he is, that might make him a good agent, who knows? If I badmouth someone, no matter how I write it, I end up looking petty.

If you read all the listings, you will have an overview. If I think someone is full of it, read carefully, you'll figure it out. I've endeavored to present the facts plus whatever might have struck me about the agent; this one is a Backgammon player and that one is a computer freak.

Some agents have survived for years without ever really representing their clients. They wait for the phone to ring. Some agents talk a better game than they play. I believe it is better to have no agent than an agent who is going to lie to you.

We all know the stereotypes about agents, *They lie, that's their job.* Well, some agents lie, but most agents don't. Most agents are hard working, professional regular people who (like you) want to make it in show business. They too, want to be respected for their work, go to the Tonys, the Academy Awards and the Emmys and get great tables at Sardi's and Spago. And they, like you, are willing to put up with the toughest, most heartbreaking business in the world because they are mavericks who love the adventure and can't think of a single thing that interests them more.

I know many who read this book are just starting out and will be scanning the agencies for those who seem to be building their lists. Many of those agents have great potential. There are some who don't.

In the past, my practice has been to personally interview every agent listed in the book, other than ICM, WMA and CAA. That's still mostly true, though in the interests of time, there are a few agents that I interviewed on the phone.

Most of the time, I went to the office because that was the most convenient for the agent and seeing the office helped me make judgments about the agency. I didn't meet everyone at every agency or all the partners, but I did meet with a partner or an agent who was acting as a spokesman for the company. I could be wrong in my judgments, but at least they are not based on hearsay.

I went through a real crisis about whom to include. Anybody who would talk to me? Only those agents that I could actually in good conscience recommend? It seems inappropriate for me to try to play God about who is worthy and who is not. On the other hand, I don't want my readers to think I would recommend everyone who is in the book. That automatically makes anyone not in the book suspect. Also, there are people who for whatever reason won't talk to me, or I just couldn't get to. I finally decided to include everyone I researched.

Agents reflect a major portion of the business. If you are currently employed in the business in any conspicuous way, people are usually nice to you and validate your existence. If you are not, the lack of respect can be appalling.

Keep your wits about you and you'll gain perspective when these same people fawn all over you once you actually do some visible work. Maybe their fawning is not just an exercise in fakery. It is true that successful people are usually sending off better vibes, although some are still stinkers.

Whether you're gainfully employed in the business or not, endeavor to keep your sense of humor handy, it will help you survive.

Some agents would not let me name any of their clients and others didn't mind if I named clients, they just didn't want to be responsible for singling any one out. As a whole, just assume that I looked up the client list plus credits and listed a few that I thought were representative of the list.

If you find an agency that seems to appeal to you, check the index in the back of the book to see if that agent has any quotes and if so, check them out. This will give you more insight.

When you query agents, be discriminating. Don't blanket the town with pictures and resumes. Target the agent that seems right for you and ration yourself. It's a better use of your energy and more likely to pay off.

Agents are inundated with pictures and resumes

and while they are all looking for the next hot actor, there are only so many hours in a day, so don't waste their time or yours. If you are just starting, don't expect ICM to come knocking at your door. Choose someone who is at the same level as you are and grow together.

If you have just gotten a job on your own, you will probably have some referrals already. Check them out and see who appeals to you. A job is not automatic entree. As you have probably noted throughout the book, most agents are not interested in a one shot deal. In my experience researching agents for actors, writers and directors, I keep learning that agents are interested in a body of work.

They want to see a progression of you and your product. They want to know that they are not squandering their hard won contacts on someone who doesn't have the ability to go the distance. They won't be able to buy a cottage in the south of France on their commissions for one job. Neither will you.

Like attracts like. You will ultimately get just what you want in an agent. I believe you can get a terrific agent. I believe you can be a terrific client. There are no shortcuts. And today is not the last day of your life. In her book, *My Lives,* Roseanne quotes a line from Sun Tzu's, *The Art of War*, which she says everyone in Hollywood has read. It says: *The one who cares most wins.*

Kevin Bacon/Referrals

As you read the agency listings, you will see that many of the agents, though they will look at pictures and resumes, are not open to being contacted by new people who have no one to recommend them. Before you wring your hands and gnash your teeth, remember The Kevin Bacon Game. It's the same concept as the play/movie *Six Degrees of Separation* which contends that anyone in the world can find an association with anyone else in the world through six associations, only in the Kevin game, it only takes three.

It goes like this. *Your mother shops at the same grocery store that Kevin Bacon does*...or in my own case, I have worked with Tom Hanks who knows Kevin Bacon, so, ostensibly, if I had a script I wanted to get to Kevin, I ought to be able to get it to him through Tom.

This all goes by way of saying that if you track all the odds and ends of your life, you should be able to produce *somebody who knows somebody who knows somebody* and come up with an authentic (however tenuous), connection to someone who can make a call for you so that you are not just querying/calling cold.

If you can't come up with a connection, you'll write the best darn letter in the world and knock some agent right on his butt, but if you can score at *the Kevin Game,* it would be best.

Check all addresses before mailing. Every effort has been made to provide accurate and current addresses and phone numbers, but agents move and computers goof. Call the office and verify the address. They won't know it's you.

✦ Remember

✓ Your first agent is yourself. You must be your own agent until you attract someone who will care and has more access than you. It's better to keep on being your own agent than to have an agent without access or passion.

✓ Make yourself read all the listings before you make a decision.

✓ Mass mailings are usually a waste of money. There is no use sending WMA or ICM a letter without entree. It's pointless to query someone you have never heard of. If you have no information about the agent, how do you know you want him? Take the long view. Look for an agent you would want to be with for years. Be selective.

✓ Don't blow your chances of being taken seriously by pursuing an agent before you are ready.

✓ Although rules were made to be broken, presuming on an agent's time by showing up at his office without an appointment or calling and asking to speak to the agent as though you are an old friend, will ultimately backfire. Observe good manners and be sensitive to other people's space and time.

✓ Getting the right agent is not the answer to all your prayers — but, it's a start!

✦ Abrams Artists & Associates, Ltd.

420 Madison Avenue S, 14th Floor
at 47th Street
New York, NY 10017
212-935-8980

A brusk, efficient man, Harry Abrams has headed or partnered a string of agencies over the years: Abrams-Rubaloff, one of *the* commercial forces in New York City in the late 1960s and 1970s, Abrams Harris & Goldberg, a prestigious theatrical agency in Los Angeles during the early to mid-1980s and currently Abrams Artists both in New York and Los Angeles. Through resourcefulness, determination and the hiring of excellent theatrical agents with their own splendid client lists, Abrams has carved out an impressive New York agency that is well thought of in all areas of the business.

Abrams runs the motion picture and television department in Los Angeles and Robert Atterman, who began his career in the mailroom at ICM, heads that department in New York. Colleagues Rob Kolker, Ellen Gilbert and Heather Collier all worked their way through the training program at Abrams Artists and join Atterman and Craig Cohen (ICM) shepherding their distinguished clients for film, theatre and television. Gilbert helms the children's division.

Agents
Robert Atterman, Rob Kolker, Ellen Gilbert,
Craig Cohen, Heather Collier and Michelle Grant
Client List
95-100
Clients
Check Screen Actors Guild listings

✦ Acme Talent & Literary

625 Broadway 8th floor
between Bleeker & Houston
New York, NY 10012
212-328-0388

Lisa Lindo Lieblein and husband Adam, opened their Los Angeles based office in 1993. When they booked 8 people onto Broadway and 2 into soaps from Los Angeles, they figured they should start a New York office and in January of 1997, they did.

Lisa began her career working for the legendary Norman Lear at Act III and was trained as an agent at The Susan Smith Agency before agenting at Triad and ICM, so it's clear that Lisa knows how to do things right.

None of that, however, prepared me for what I consider to be the most creative accomplishment in her background, creating The Fifth Network.

The Network was a group of working industry folk who wanted to make a difference. For several years, a core group of 600 met monthly for a sit-down dinner to discuss how they could influence the business in a positive way. The group no longer meets, but the thought, energy and organizational skills required to bring off such a feat, makes me certain that anything Lisa sets out to do will become reality.

Adam Lieblein is no slouch either. He began as a production assistant on commercials, ultimately becoming a production coordinator, a production manager and finally a producer for Bob Giraldi, Koppos, Propaganda and other big commercial production companies.

Between them, Lisa and Adam were brilliantly equipped to start either their own production company or talent agency. With no project to produce that interested them, the merger between Triad and William Morris afforded them the opportunity to open their own agency with an enviable client list of Triad orphans.

The New York theatrical list includes names like Ethan Erickson (*Guiding Light*), Jason Hayes (*Vampires*), Marc Schwarz (*Vampires*), Judy McLane, Joel Robertson and Sondra Grant and has about 30 other actors all working on Broadway. Rodney Ferrell shepherds the theatrical clients, including children, with Eileen Haves in charge of the commercial department.

Although Acme looks at pictures and resumes, clients come chiefly through industry referral.

The agency represents writers, comedians, and actors, young adults, teenagers and children.

Agents
Lisa Lindo Lieblein and Rodney Ferrell
Client list
50
Clients
Ethan Erickson, Jason Hayes, Marc Schwarz,
Judy McLane, Joel Robertson, Sondra Grant and others

✦ Bret Adams

448 W 44th Street
btwn 9th & 10th Avenues
New York, NY 10036
212-765-5630

If it's a job in the theatre, Bret Adams has probably done it. The number of things that Bret has found a way to make money from in the business is a testimony to his creativity and resourcefulness.

Even when renting binoculars at the theatre while trying to make ends meet as an actor, fate smiled on Bret, for producers saw him at the theatre so regularly, they thought Bret was just a conscientious actor studying his craft!

Bret worked in movies and off Broadway before he decided to work as an agent for no salary in order to learn the business. While partnered with Sanford Leigh, he represented Ina Balin, Tippi Hedrin and Ellen Burstyn as they were all beginning their careers. He moved to Australia trying his hand at producing, creating an *artistically successful though financially shaky theatre.*

From acting to producing to publicity and stage managing for Equity, Bret cut a varied path to his life today as one of the most reputable independent agents in New York at the agency he founded in 1971.

Colleague Margi Roundtree has been with Bret for years. In addition to their superior skills at agenting, I have it on good authority that both Margi and Bret are both ace Backgammon players.

Ken Melamed (Honey Sanders, Monty Silver) joins Bret and Margi repping clients like Judy Kaye, Ron Holgate, John James, Noel Harrison, Millicent Martin, Kenneth Haigh and Valerie Perrine.

This agency sees new clients mainly by referrals but they do check all pictures and resumes.

Agents
Bret Adams, Margi Roundtree and Ken Melamed
Client List
About 100
Clients
Judy Kaye, Ron Holgate, John James, Noel Harrison, Millicent Martin, Kenneth Haigh, Valerie Perrine and others

✦ AFA/Agents for the Arts

203 W 23rd Street, 3rd floor
btwn 7th & 8th Avenues
New York, NY 10011
212-229-2562

Quadruple threat actress-singer-production-stage-manager-director Carole Russo, arrived in New York ready for work as a performer, but quickly realized she didn't have the emotional stamina for it. She chose the next best thing and uses her background to represent and nurture her list of clients.

Carole represented models at Paul Wagner Agency and other modeling agencies before realizing that there were more creative ways to use her theatre background.

When she switched to the theatrical arena, her mentor was Fifi Oscard for whom she worked for five years. Carole has about 45 signed clients, but works with freelance actors as well.

Agents
Carole Russo
Client List
45
Clients
Jack Dabdoub, Edmund Lyndeck, Liz McConahay, Paul Jackel, David Jordan, Tommy Bull, Janet Aldrich and others

✦ Agency for the Collaborative Arts

132 W 22nd Street, 4th floor
between 6th and 7th Avenues
New York, NY 10011
212-807-8344

Nanci Brown was a film major at NYU with an eye toward going into production when she took a job interning at The Gersh Agency. Although the idea of being an agent had never occurred to her, she enjoyed the experience so much that after graduation, when Bob Barry (Barry Haft Brown) approached her about becoming his assistant, they both decided to *try it for a while and see how it went.*

It went very well since Nanci progressed from assistant to associate to partner in time for her 22nd birthday. Unfortunately Nanci's trek to Los Angeles to open BHB's LA office coincided with the big earthquake and Nanci never really felt comfortable there so after three years, she returned to New York. She did manage to bring a little of California back with her because the look of Nanci's office is very California: light and airy.

She opened her own office in 1995. Representative of her list of 60 clients are Elisabeth Rohm (*One Life to Life*), Ben Jorgensen (*All My Children*), Kim Cea (*Smoky Joe's Café*) and Ron Bagden (Stanley, My Night with Rege). Nanci doesn't seek commercials but will handle them for a client if there is a request.

Agents
Nanci Brown
Client List
60
Clients
Elisabeth Rohm, Ben Jorgensen, Kim Cea, Ron Bagden and others

✦ Alliance Talent Inc.

1501 Broadway, #404
btwn 43rd & 44th Streets
New York, NY 10036
212-840-6868

Alliance Talent is the mid-size agency that
resulted from the merger of two of New York's brightest
and most effective agencies. Allen Flannagan of The
Allen Flannagan Agency (originally partnered with the
late Michael Kingman) and Craig Dorfman of The New
York Agency. Craig was a company manager and a
general manager before he became a franchised agent at
The Leaverton Agency. Flannagan and Dorfman
collaborated to form what has become a distinguished
agency respected by casting directors and producers alike.

Flannagan, thought of as a balancing personality
with a great eye for talent when he was in business with
Michael Kingman, is now the head of the New York
office since Dorfman went West to open the Los Angeles
office in 1994. Carol Davis is Allen's colleague at ATI.

Agents
Allen Flannagan and Carol Davis
Client List
100
Clients
S. Epatha Merkerson, Savion Glover and others

✦ American International Talent Agency

303 W 42ⁿᵈ Street # 608
between 8ᵗʰ & 9ᵗʰ Avenues
New York, NY 10019
212-664-0641

Wanza and Claretta King have been in the business *all their lives*. Actors and singers, they were seeking a way to stay in the business when they hit upon the idea of starting their own theatrical agency. Since it's been 30 years, I guess it worked!

The Kings work with about 30 signed and a large list of freelance actors, comedians, dancers, choreographers, musical artists, young adults, teenagers, variety and voice-over artists.

AIT also handles international companies of hit musicals requiring performers fluent in other languages. They book cruise ships so if you are interested in putting your club act together, American International might be the agency to contact.

Clients from their signed list include Sandra Grant (*One Life to Live*), Daryl Young, Phyllis Thornton and William Robinson.

This agency books for theatre, film, television, commercials, voice-overs and special events.

Agents
Claretta King and Wanza King
Client List
30 plus freelance
Clients
Sandra Grant, Daryl Young, Phyllis Thornton, William Robinson and others

✦ Beverly Anderson

1501 Broadway, # 2008
btwn 43rd & 44th Streets
New York, NY 10036
212-944-7773

Colorful, candid Beverly Anderson was an actress herself until she tired of life on the road. Her agenting career began in 1956 at Dale Garrick Modeling. At Garrick, which was a models-only agency, Beverly suggested checking out some of the beauties to see if they could talk a bit and qualify for The Jackie Gleason and Steve Allen shows.

She ended up booking consistently and joined Jan Welsh (an Equity agent), where her first submission placed Earl Sindor into a classic of the American Theatre, *Sweet Bird of Youth*.

Some of Beverly's clients include Jennifer Piech (*Titanic, Dellaventura*), Robert Ousley and Tim Howard (*Showboat*), and Kathryn Crosby who is currently playing *The Music Man* abroad.

Beverly Anderson earns the bulk of her money as one of the key agents in Manhattan for the musical theatre. Her list of signed clients is short, but she works extensively with freelance talent.

Beverly has had her own agency for over 25 years and says that she is currently enjoying *the longest run of any lone female agency owner in New York!* She constantly attends showcases always on the lookout for new young actors and she says that her greatest thrill is developing the careers of young artists.

Agents
Beverly Anderson
Client List
15 + freelance
Clients
Jennifer Piech, Robert Ousley, Tim Howard,
Kathryn Crosby and others

✦ Andreadis Talent Agency, Inc.

119 West 57th Street, #711
E of 7th Avenue
New York, NY 10019
212-315-0303

Like many actresses, Barbara Andreadis left the
business when she had children. The kids are grown now
but instead of continuing her earlier life as an actress,
Barbara is continuing as a mother. This time, however,
she has a larger family — of actors who, of course will
always need her. When she decided to return to the
business as an agent, Barbara trained at Bonni Kidd. She
ended up running the agency for two years before
starting her own business in 1983.

Barbara says she carries no generic type, *only
individuals* and has clients on soaps as well as on
Broadway and in film and television. Barbara has strong
representation on Broadway in musical theatre.

Representative clients include Eileen Fulton (*As
the World Turns*), Jacob Brent (*Cats*), Billy Hufsey (*Fame*),
Greg Butler (*Chicago*), Chance Kelly (*New York Undercover,
Puppet*), James Bohanek (the Elliot Ness project), Penny
Ayn Maas (*Crazy for You*), Greg Ramos (*West Side Story*),
Daniel Musico (*Hell's Kitchen*) Karen Lynn Gorney
(*Saturday Night Fever*), Robert Jensen (*Secret Garden*),
Timothy Blevins and Jill Nicklaus.

As you can see from the credits above, Barbara is
establishing a reputation for good musical talent. She
usually sees people only by referral, but does look at all
pictures and resumes.

Agents
Barbara Andreadis
Client List
15 + freelance
Clients
Eileen Fulton, Penny Ayn Maas, Robert Jensen, Timothy
Blevins, Jill Nicklaus, Billy Hufsey, Karen Lynn Gorney,
Jacob Brent, James Bohanek, Greg Butler, Chance Kelly,
Greg Ramos, Daniel Musico and others

✦ APA/Agency for the Performing Arts

888 7th Avenue
btwn 56th & 56th Streets
New York, NY 10106
212-582-1500

Founded in the 1960s by expatriates of MCA/ICM, APA is the smallest of the corporate agencies. Because the size of the client list allows a more hands on approach, agents at APA are able to take the access that comes from servicing actors, writers, directors, producers, stand-up performers, newscasters, concert performers, etc. and nourish clients with the kind of attention one would usually only expect to get from an independent agent.

President David Baumgarten and theatrical department head, Harvey Litwin (MCA) have both been with APA from the beginning. Their crew of agents includes Matthew Sullivan, who graduated from the agent-training-program at APA, Maryanne Rubacky (Michael Hartig) and Lorraine Coffey (Bob MacGowan Management).

Representative of the combined New York/Los Angeles client list are Ian Ziering, Judd Hirsh, Bai Ling, James Duvall, Chris Eigeman, Jamie Kennedy, Rita Moreno, Swoozsie Kurtz and Phylicia Rashad.

In addition to APA's illustrious strong list of acting clients, the agency is also known as the place for comedy development and regularly holds its own showcases to introduce clients to buyers.

Because APA needs to try harder, they do, developing talent, checking out the town and returning phone calls.

Agents
Harvey Litwin, Matthew Sullivan, Maryanne Rubacky and
Lorraine Coffey
Client List
250 combined NY/LA list
Clients
Ian Ziering, Rita Moreno, Swoozsie Kurtz, Bai Ling,
Phylicia Rashad, James Duvall, Jamie Kennedy,
Chris Eigeman, Judd Hirsh and others

✦ Artists Group East

1650 Broadway, #711
at 51st Street
New York, NY 10019
212-586-1452

In November of 1996, The Actor's Group (Pat House) and The Artists Group East (Robert Malcolm) merged their offices. They could have called themselves The Actors/Artists Group, but decided to just adapt the name that Robert Malcolm adopted when he merged his New York agency (PGA, Inc.) with the prestigious west coast Artists Group in 1993.

Robert has been dividing his time between New York and Los Angeles ever since that merger. In 1996, Robert decided it was time to turn over the New York office to a someone with a stake in the business. He couldn't have chosen a better person than Pat House.

Pat's 1968 decision to give up acting and join Stewart Artists, representing then models-becoming-actors Cybil Shepherd, Susan Dey and others, was just the beginning of a career spent nurturing actors. She worked with both Wilhelmina and Harry Abrams before joining Michael Slessinger at The Actors Group in 1982. Michael was another partner who moved to the west coast so in 1990, Michael sold the New York part of the business and the name to Pat.

Now Pat has a new name and a new partner and couldn't be happier. Her list of steadily working clients grows more and more visible with Susan Wood currently working in *Ragtime* in Los Angeles, Tommy Hollis (*The Piano, Seven Guitars*) just finishing up his work in Mike Nichols' new film, *Primary Colors* and client, Marylouise Burke is working with Anthony Hopkins and Brad Pitt in the new film, *Meet Joe Black*.

Cynthia Katz (Abrams Artists), who has worked with Robert for many years is now Pat's colleague.

Agents
Pat House and Cynthia Katz
Client List
65
Clients
Susan Wood, Tommy Hollis, Marylouise Burke and others

✦ Richard Astor

250 W 57th Street, #2014
at Broadway
New York, NY 10107
212-581-1970

An old-line class-act, Richard Astor is one of my favorites. I remember how nice he was to me when I came in off the street as a beginning actor to drop off a picture and resume. The man has stature, access, taste and a keen eye for talent; Martin Sheen, Gene Hackman, Robert Duvall and Nell Carter are only a few of the actors represented by Richard early in their careers.

Richard began as an actor in 1957, but a work-related back injury forced him to leave acting, so New York State's Workman's Compensation trained him for a new profession. Since Richard knew he wanted to be an agent, he chose typing and speed writing.

He assisted agent, Henry C. Brown and then worked for Lily Veidt and Harriet Kaplan before opening his own agency in 1960.

This office accepts resumes via referral only, and constantly tracks actors via showcases and workshops. If you do the work, they will find you. Freelance at this agency is only a first step toward signing and is a very limited practice.

Agent wanna-bes should look to this office for help as this agency routinely hires interns interested in learning the business of the business.

Agents
Richard Astor
Client List
40
Clients
Danny Aiello, Rutanya Alda and others

✦ Bauman Hiller & Associates

250 W 57th Street, Penthouse 5
at Broadway
New York, NY 10107
212-757-0098

The style of this respected old-line agency on both coasts is comfortable and easy. Serious about business and light-hearted about life, West Coast partners Dick Bauman and Wally Hiller have chosen affable Mark Redanty to head the New York office. Mark got his first taste of the business when he interned at Ragland-Shamsky while he was in college. After he completed his education, he pursued other things before the lure of show business called him back to work with Richard Astor.

Mark has been the head of the New York office of Bauman Hiller & Associates since 1987. He and colleague David Shaul (Henderson Hogan) preside over an important and respected list of clients.

Some clients from their list include Victoria Clark (*The Titanic*), Mark Kudisch (*Beauty and the Beast, High Society*), Peter Scolari, Donna McKechnie, William Katt, Glynnis O'Connor, Robert Morse, Sada Thompson, Scott Wise, Peter Frechette, Teresa Merritt, David Drake, James Earl Jones and Dennis Parlato and Justin Deas who are on *The Guiding Light*.

Bauman Hiller & Associates work freelance only as a prelude to signing.

Agents
Mark Redanty and David Shaul
Client List
80
Clients
Robert Morse, Sada Thompson, Scott Wise,
Peter Frechette, Teresa Merritt, David Drake, Donna
McKechnie, Peter Scolari, William Katt, Glynnis
O'Connor, James Earle Jones, Victoria Clark, Mark
Kudisch, Dennis Parlato, Justin Deas and others

✦ Barry Haft Brown

165 W 46th Street, #2223
btwn 6th & 7th Avenues
New York, NY 10019
212-869-9310

Barry Haft Brown is one of the most productive agencies in town. Bob Barry maintained The Barry Agency for 33 years until late 1991, when Bob, whose discerning eye uncovered former clients Gene Hackman, Willem Dafoe, Christopher Walken, Scott Glenn, Maureen Stapleton and Harvey Kietel, joined colleagues Steven Haft (Ambrosio/Mortimer) and Nanci Brown (The Gersh Agency) to form BHB.

Brown and Haft have now moved on, but Bob continues to run the kind of discriminating agency that casting directors consult regularly.

Former actor Meg Pantera changed sides of the desk and now joins Bob repping the 75-80 clients at this agency. Clients include James Hanlon (*Brooklyn South*), Bryant Carroll (*Footloose*), Gordon MacDonald (*The Thin Red Line*), Louise Sorel (*One Life to Live*), Michelle Robinson (*Chicago*), Tracy Chapman (*The Lion King*) and Clark Thorell and Lisa Datz who are both in *The Titanic*.

BHB's clients work in the theatre, films, soaps, and in all areas of television. This agency only works with signed clients.

Agents
Bob Barry and Meg Pantera
Client List
75-80
Clients
James Hanlon, Louise Sorel, Bryant Carroll, Lisa Datz, Michelle Robinson, Tracy Chapman, Clark Thorell, Gordon MacDonald and others

✦ Peter Beilin Agency, Inc.

230 Park Avenue, #923
across from the Pan Am Building
New York, NY 10169
212-949-9119

Peter Beilin was my commercial agent years ago at Abrams-Rubaloff. A talented and determined man, I was not surprised that he started his own agency when A-R split in 1977. What *did* surprise me is that in the corner of Peter's office, his old Rolodex was still in tact. He still had my old New York phone number! Peter is obviously a man who throws nothing away and is ready for everything.

A musician afraid that choosing music as his livelihood would diminish its joy for him, Peter started off working as a page at ABC. He quickly became the Night Program Manager: *The guy they leave in charge when the important people go home.* He produced for a while before crossing paths with Noel Rubaloff who inspired him to become an agent.

PBA looks for multi-talented performers. This agency's client roster includes professional athletes, sportscasters, radio and television personalities and stand-up comedians for both television and commercials.

Agents
Peter Beilin
Client List
Freelance
Clients
Freelance

✦ The Bethel Agencies

360 W 53rd Street, #BA
just E of 9th Avenue
New York NY 10019
212-664-0455

Lewis Chambers worked in Admissions at Roosevelt Hospital before fate intervened introducing him to the world of photographers and their agents. When he opened his own agency three years later, he began making deals even before he had time to name his agency. Concluding negotiation on a deal and pressed for a name, he decided on the spot to name his agency for a small town just south of his home town of Randolph, Vermont.

This was back in December, 1967 when The Bethel Agency represented only photojournalists. Within six months they began representing writers and among other prestigious works, sold *Auditioning for the Musical Theatre* as well as one of the best books an actor could ever buy — Michael Shurtleff's *Audition.*

On the agency's 15th birthday in 1982, Lewis expanded the agency's client list to include actors. Today he maintains an emphasis on actors, playwrights, writers of non-fiction and novelists. Bethel's actors work in all areas — theatre, film and television. He also occasionally represents actors for commercials.

In addition to this agency, Lewis partners with Norma Liebert, The Norma-Lewis Agency, to sell children's books. That's why it's called the Bethel Agenc*ies*.

Agents
Lewis Chambers
Clients List
75 signed + freelance
Clients
Thomas Barbour, Vera Johnson, Katherine Harber,
Ronald L. Brown, Mary Leigh Stahl, Mary Daciuk,
Margot White, Mary Jasperson, Nan Wilson and others

✦ Berman, Boals and Flynn, Inc.

225 Lafayette Street, #1207
S of Houston/E of Broadway
New York, NY 10012
212-966-0339

Jim Flynn entered show business by answering
phones for Susan Smith at her agency in 1990. His first
agenting job was at The New York Agency which merged
with Alliance Talent. In 1995, he teamed up with literary
legends Lois Berman and Judy Boals to create one of the
most effective agencies in town.

A conscious decision to limit their client list to
those actors, writers, composers/songwriters and
directors who are not only talented, but easy to get along
with has resulted in an agency that feels like a very happy
family.

Though Jim Flynn heads the theatrical side of the
business and Judy is the literary chief, he still handles the
literary clients he brought with him. Charles Grayauski
brings his background as an actor and restaurant manager
to his role as head of the emerging commercial division at
BB&F.

Judy Boals also started in the business as an
actor. A part-time job working with Lois Berman in
varying capacities ultimately led to her agenting career.
With the birth of Berman, Boals and Flynn, Judy is now
her former mentor's partner. Berman functions as a silent
partner and consultant.

BB&F's list of actors includes Tom O'Leary,
Tom Ryan, David Greenspan, Rickie Cost, Carolyn Swift
and Priscilla Shanks. Their clients come to them either
through referrals or the agents find them in showcases.

There are good quotes from Judy and Jim
elsewhere in the book. Although this office looks at all
pictures and resumes, they rarely call anyone in from

them.

Agents
Jim Flynn, Judy Boals and Charles Grayauski
Client List
50
Clients
Tom O'Leary, Tom Ryan, David Greenspan, Rickie Cost, Carolyn Swift, Priscilla Shanks and others

✦ Big Duke 6 Artists Inc.

5 Union Square W
14th Street, 5th floor
New York, NY 10003
212-989-6927

Mike Casey has an eye for beauty and talent. Founder of Flick (1985), Despointes-Casey (1989) and now Big Duke 6 Artists, Inc., Mike has a way of picking winners. His ability to choose and nurture performers with career potential and has earned him great respect.

Flick became the place to be when Mike helped make actors like Isabella Rosselini, Uma Thurman, David Duchovny, Juliana Marguiles and Kelly Lynch visible personas, but wishing to have more control, Mike took Kelly and Juliana and along with a French partner, started Despointes-Casey. When the agency moved to Paris, Mike decided to take a breather from the business.

It didn't take long for Mike to miss his calling, so this time, in addition to having a cool agency, Mike is fulfilling a fantasy and naming his business after Robert Duvall's helicopter in *Apocalypse Now.*

Big Duke 6 has 12 actors for film and 7 for soaps. Mike only represents clients for film, commercials and contract roles for soaps. He does not book day players and has no interest in theatre or prime-time television.

In addition to repping actors, Mike represents a list of 45 NFL football players for commercials, ice-skater Katerina Vitt, swimmer, Amanda Beard, boxers Andrew Golota, Ray Mercer and Shannon Biggs and a host of other sports personalities.

Two from his list of beautiful actress/models are Maria Holvoe (*3 Men & and a Baby*) and newcomer Ekeda Feingold.

Agents
Mike Casey
Client List
12
Clients
Maria Holvoe, Ekeda Feingold and others

✦ J. Michael Bloom & Associates

233 Park Avenue S, 10th Floor
at 19th Street
New York, NY 10003
212-529-5800/212-529-8514

An actor himself once, J. Michael Bloom is a flamboyant individual whom I have always found to be both fair and candid. The commercial arm of this brilliant office has long been a mainstay on the New York scene, but the impressive list of movie stars that Michael and colleagues have found and nurtured has made JMB a force to be reckoned with in New York or Los Angeles.

Though Michael spends most of his time in California, he is hands-on to important clients on either coast. The New York theatrical department is headed by Philip Carlson.

Like Michael, Philip was also a working actor who felt the pull from the other side of the table. His job working in management at Curtis Brown merely whet his appetite. Feeling that he wanted to be more aggressive for his clients, Philip left managing to become an agent. He worked at both Susan Smith and Writers & Artists before aligning with J. Michael in 1996.

Caroline Daughters (Harter Manning Woo) and Mark Schlegel (Ambrosio Mortimer) join Philip in repping clients like Rob Campbell, Lois Smith, Colm Feore, Lanie Kazan, Lori Petty, Marianne Jean-Baptiste, Alex Kingston, Trini Alvarado, Barnard Hughes and Anthony Heald.

J. Michael Bloom & Associates is an important liaison to the British marketplace representing not only British stars in America, but providing a liaison between American clients and British representation.

The physical splendor of this office is impressive. I can imagine an actor dutifully interviewing agents and reviewing data in order to make an intelligent decision and then getting off the elevator, taking one look at the sumptuousness of the office and at Michael's name in 12-foot-tall letters (only a slight exaggeration), holding out his pictures and saying, *Sign me*. Luckily, this office also has credibility, a great list and terrific agents.

Both the adult and youth legit departments haunt showcases, schools and the local theatrical scene, on the lookout for talent in all age ranges.

Agents
Philip Carlson, Mark Schlegel and Caroline Daughters
Client List
80
Clients
Rob Campbell, Lois Smith, Colm Feore, Lanie Kazan, Lori Petty, Marianne Jean-Baptiste, Alex Kingston, Trini Alvarado, Barnard Hughes, Anthony Heald and others

✦ Don Buchwald & Associates

10 E 44th Street
just E of 5th Avenue
New York, NY 10017
212-867-1070

Ex-actor/producer Don Buchwald got his first job agenting with Monty Silver in 1964. He ran his own agency (Don Buchwald) before joining the prestigious commercial agency, Abrams-Rubaloff in 1971. His experience with A-R led to his new agency, Don Buchwald & Associates, when A-R split.

A brilliant negotiator and a shrewd agent, Buchwald has built an impressive list of clients *and* agents headed by Vice-President of Corporate Affairs, attorney, Richard Basch. Other Buchwald theatrical agents are Ricki Olshan, David Williams, Kristin Miller, Joanne Nici and David Williams.

I've been spare talking about this agency just because I can't get anyone there to return my phone calls in order to update my information. Don't misconstrue my brevity. This is a class agency.

There is also a Los Angeles office to help represent such prestigious clients as Florence Stanley, Louise Fletcher, Jay Thomas, Irene Bedard, Jay Sanders and De Lane Matthews.

Agents
Don Buchwald, Richard Basch, Ricki Olshan, Kristin Miller, Joanne Nici and David Williams
Client List
100-150
Clients
Florence Stanley, Irene Bedard, Louise Fletcher, Jay Sanders, De Lane Matthews, Jay Thomas and others

✦ Carry Company Talent Representatives

1501 Broadway, #1408
btwn 43rd & 44th Streets
New York, NY 10036
212-768-2793

Sharon Carry experienced and witnessed actor/agent and actor/casting director relationships as an actor. When she changed sides of the desk, she decided there *must be a better way of interaction* and vowed to make the business of acting a little less painful.

Her first priority as an agent was to make sure the actors were treated with respect. From the care exhibited toward clients when I was in their office, Sharon is definitely putting her plan into action.

Her agency represents ethnics, children, babies, athletes, stand-ups, actors and models. The Carry Company was established in early 1991 with Sharon's agent training coming from the modeling/print side of the business.

The Carry Company concentrates on their signed clients, but also works on a freelance basis.

Colleague, Marcia Tovsky spent 15 years working in the television industry. Prior to joining CC, she was a celebrity talent coordinator, a special events producer and also worked for ABC and Nickelodeon. Marcia heads the commercial department.

The Carry Company has a pool of about 50 kids and 50 adults. Don't postcard this agency unless you have something real to say, *Hello, how are you?* doesn't count. They prefer flyers when you are doing something. The Carry Company takes flyers and work very seriously.

Agents
Sharon Carry
Client List
100
Clients
Check Screen Actor Guild listings

✦ Carson-Adler Agency, Inc.

250 W 57th Street
at Broadway
New York, NY 10107
212-541-7008

One of the most respected children's agencies in New York is run by former showbiz mom, Nancy Carson. Being a stage mother showed her a side of the business most agents never experience and inspired her to start an agency where children would be protected.

She learned the agent side of the biz at the prestigious children's agency, Jan J. before joining with Marion Adler to form C-A in 1982. Marion passed away in 1993.

Shirley Faison is now Nancy's colleague in the children's theatrical division. In addition to her background in management at the National Black Theatre, Shirley is also the mother of successful child actors, so, like Nancy, she intimately understands the challenges of her clients and their parents.

The successful commercial division is run by ex-child actor Bonnie Deroski who thought she really wanted to leave the business, but finds that this is where her heart lies.

This office is clearly the place casting directors shop for talented, trained, young legit actors. Their roster includes Alexander Goodwin (*Nobody's Fool, Mimic, Box of Moonlight, I'm Not Rappaport*), Bobby McAdams (*Minor Adjustments*), Leelee Sobieski (*Jungle to Jungle, Deep Impact, A Soldier's Daughter Never Cries*), Steve Pasquale (*Miss Saigon*) Jessica Grove (*Miss Saigon, The Wizard of Oz*), Michael Parducci (*Gravesend*), Jessie Lee (*The Brady Bunch*), Brittany Walsh (*The Sound of Music*), Alison Folland (*All Over Me, To Die For, Before and After*), Donald Faison (*Clueless, Waiting to Exhale*), Frankie Galasso (*Jungle to*

Jungle, Hudson Street, Oliver), Taryn Davis (*Snow White: A Tale of Terror*), Lauren Pratt *(Object of My Affection, Second Day of Christmas)* and David Krumholt (*The Santa Clause, The Ice Storm, Adams Family Values*).

The agency has 75 signed clients for theatre, film, and television. Carson-Adler looks at all pictures. They need not be professionally done to be considered.

Nancy has written the definitive *How To* book for young actors and their moms seeking work in the business, *Kid Biz*. It's available at most bookstores and libraries. It answers almost any question you might have about children in the business. I highly recommend it.

Agents
Nancy Carson and Shirley Faison
Client List
60
Clients
Alexander Goodwin, Bobby McAdams, David Krumholt, Brittany Walsh, Donald Faison, Frankie Galasso, Jessie Lee, Jessica Grove, Lauren Pratt, Leelee Sobieski, Michael Parducci, Allison Folland, Steve Pasquale, Taryn Davis and others

✦ The Carson Organization

Helen Hayes Theatre Building
240 W 44th Street, PH
btwn Broadway & 8th Avenue
New York, NY 10036
212-221-1517

Steve Carson and wife, Maria Burton-Carson opened The Carson Organization in late 1992 and from the looks of things, this agency is going to be around for a long time. As the daughter of Elizabeth Taylor and Richard Burton, Maria brings a certain overview to the business, and Steve's background at New York agencies (Gilchrist, Phoenix, etc.) combine to make this agency a good choice for actors under age 30 who are looking for a home. Although Steve, Maria and colleague Barry Kolker (Fifi Oscard) do represent the occasional freelance actor, their commitment is to their signed clients.

Names from their list include Chaz Shepherd (*Me and the Boys*), Merlin Santana (*Under One Roof, Steve Harvey Show*), Will Friedle (*Boy Meets World, The King & I*), Dion Collins (*Ragtime*), Sharon Leal (*The Guiding Light*), Andrew Levitas (*Nick Freno*), Tristen Mays (*Gullah Gullah Island*), Alaine Kashian (*Carmen San Diego*) James Van Der Beek (*Angus Bethune*), Siri Howard (*The Sound of Music*), Shawn Thompson (*The Heights*) and Jesse Cameron (*Slaughter of the Innocents*).

This agency handles children, but not infants. Steve says they look at all pictures and resumes and have found some of the most important people on his list from the mail.

Agents

Steve Carson, Maria Burton-Carson and Barry Kolker

Client List

80 + very little freelance

Clients

Merlin Santana, Will Friedle, Chaz Shepherd,
Shawn Thompson, Jesse Cameron, Andrew Levitas,
Tristen Mays, Dion Collins, Sharon Leal, Alaine Kashian,
James Van Der Beek, Siri Howard and others

✦ Coleman-Rosenberg

155 E 55th Street, Room 5D
btwn Lexington & 3rd Avenues
New York, NY 10022
212-838-0734

Deborah Coleman and Jack Rosenberg started this agency in the 1950s to represent actors, writers, directors and choreographers.. This small anonymous agency purposefully manages to remain so, though their clients are distinguished and visible.

Because the list is intentionally small, clients receive close attention and nurturing.

Names from their list include Jean Stapleton and Gerald Freedman. C-R looks at all pictures and resumes but prefers (as do most agents) to choose their clients by seeing them work.

Agents
Deborah Coleman
Client List
35-40
Clients
Jean Stapleton, Austin Pendelton, Donald Sadler, Gerald Freedman and others

✦ DGRW/Douglas, Gorman, Rothacker & Wilhelm, Inc.

1501 Broadway, #703
btwn 43rd & 44th Streets
New York, NY 10036
212-382-2000

Flo Rothacker (Ann Wright), Jim Wilhelm (Lionel Larner, Eric Ross, The Barry Douglas Agency), Barry Douglas (ICM) and Fred Gorman (Bret Adams) created this effective, congenial agency in 1988.

Barry and Fred died in 1996, but the partners worked diligently to make sure that the agency survived the sad changes. Today DGRW is a strong as ever, and continuing to diversify and expand their client list.

Although this agency has grown in stature and access, it has not sacrificed the nurturing elements that made it special to actors in the first place. Flo Rothacker still has the sensibilities that made her choose her first job at Ann Wright's agency due to its proximity to Bloomingdales and she endures as one of New York's major musical comedy agents. Flo is quoted at length throughout the book.

Jim Wilheim has done everything. Beginning in the business when he was fifteen years old, he has worked as an actor, stage manager, public relations director, general manager and casting director before becoming an agent in 1981. He has a stellar reputation in New York working with diverse and well respected actors — especially in concerts, on network television and in major features.

In addition to all his other activities, Jim finds time to function on the guest faculty at University of Cincinnati/College Conservatory of Music, journeying there five times a year to guide new students and stage productions.

Agent/lawyer Andy Lawler who graduated from the University of North Carolina Chapel Hill, Beth Schacter, who was a producer at Williamstown, and Michelle Gerard, all went through the agent-training program at DGRW and now join Flo and Jim in representing the 100 or so clients on their list.

Names from their list include Harold Perrineau (*Romeo & Juliet, Smoke, The Edge*), Kathleen Chalfant (*Angels in America*), Harry Groener (*Crazy for You*), Kristen Wilson (*Dr. Doolittle*), Reginald Vel Johnson (*Family Matters*), Brian Stokes Mitchell (*Ragtime*), Alice Ripley (*Sideshow*) Dan Lauria (*The Wonder Years*), Sara Botsford, Marcia Mitzman, Olivia De Havilland, Laurie Beechman, superstar fight director, Rick Sordelet and others.

DGRW also represents writers, directors, fight directors, choreographers and musical directors. Clients of this office who travel west to work are introduced to several agencies with whom the office has relationships. That way the actor and the agent have a chance to make the most compatible relationship.

DGRW sees new clients through referral only although they do carefully study pictures and resumes. They are not interested in tapes produced for audition purposes only.

Agents
Jim Wilhelm, Flo Rothacker, Andy Lawler, Beth Schacter and Michelle Gerard
Client List
100
Clients
Sara Botsford, Kathleen Chalfant, Harry Groener, Kristen Wilson, Dan Lauria, Reginald Vel Johnson, Olivia De Havilland, Harold Perrineau, Alice Ripley, Brian Stokes Mitchell, Marcia Mitzman, Rick Sordelet, Laurie Beechman and others

✦ Duva - Flack Associates, Inc.

200 W 57th Street, #407
just W of 7th Avenue
New York, NY 10019
212-957-9600

A blind date for agents? Well, sorta. Elin Flack
and Bob Duva had known each other as competitors for
15 years when a friend who knew each was exploring new
paths in the business suggested they meet. Although
skeptical, each turned out to be happily surprised at how
well they meshed.

When Bob was an actor back in 1976, he asked
his agent at Talent Associates if he could be her assistant
instead of her client and since he started making deals
almost immediately, his acting days were over. Bob
agented with Mort Schwartz before he acquired a select
list of dancers and became a manager. (He booked 14 of
the 18 dancers in Bob Fosse's *Dancin'*).

Bob returned to agenting with Lionel Larner for
a year before he opened his own agency in 1982. Two
years later he was working for the most admired agent in
town, Robby Lantz.

In 1986 Bob joined The Gersh Agency New
York. He left GANY in 1992 thinking he had left the
business for good. Old friend Lantz offered him an office
while he sorted through his thoughts and feelings about
the next step.

Flack's show-biz career began because Don
Buchwald (her then-husband's employer) suggested that
she would make a great agent.

She learned the business initially from Lionel
Larner who started her as a secretary before promoting
her to agent status. She worked with LL for three years
before moving over to Harry Abrams in 1981. Her
successor at LL was Bob. Since they were traveling some

of the same roads, it's probably not too surprising that they ended up as partners.

During her six years at Harry Abrams, Elin headed up the theatrical department. She spent another six years with J. Michael Bloom where Michael's lucrative commercial business gave him the luxury of allowing his agents to nourish and develop young talent.

Like Bob, Elin left her job with no future plans — and like Bob — all her clients said, *Wherever you go, whatever you do, we want to do it with you.*

These two tasteful, connected agents have created an elegant agency to represent actors, writers, directors, director/choreographers and designers.

Even though their client list in every discipline is stellar, they do still take the time to start young artists or jump-start careers that are stalled.

They find new clients via canvassing the leagues as well as being vigilant at showcases.

Duva Flack moved to larger quarters and have added two new agents, Steven Stone (The Gersh Agency) and Richard Fisher (J. Michael Bloom) to help them represent clients like Joseph Fiennes, Ron Leibman, Boyd Gaines, Terrence Mann, Sir Alec Guinness, Patti LuPone, Mercedes Ruehl, Carole Shelley and Denny Dillon.

Agents
Robert Duva, Elin Flack, Steven Stone and Richard Fisher
Client List
65
Clients
Joseph Fiennes, Ron Leibman, Terrence Mann, Boyd Gaines, Sir Alec Guinness, Patti LuPone, Mercedes Ruehl, Carole Shelley, Denny Dillon and others

✦ Eastwood Talent Group

44 W 24th Street
W of 5th Avenue
New York NY 10010
212-645-2500

Eastwood Talent Group owner Bruce Kivo was a trainer at a health club when clients Sylvester Stallone, Rodney Dangerfield and Otto Preminger sparked his interest in show business. Originally working as an actor in commercials and films, Kivo's goal was to open his own health club in tandem with a modeling agency.

In 1982, life intruded on his plans when both his parents died. After a year of recovering, Bruce realized half his dream, opening his own modeling agency, Slique.

In 1992, he acquired backers enabling him to enlarge the agency to include actors and sports figures. At that time he changed the name to reflect the location of his office which was on the East Side.

Eastwood works with a talent pool of about 200 freelancers and about 6 signed clients.

Agents
Bruce Kivo
Client List
6 +freelance
Clients
Carol Shaya, Arthur Nascarella, Paul Greco and others

✦ Epstein-Wyckoff & Associates

311 W 43rd Street, #1401
btwn 8th & 9th Avenues
New York, NY 10036
212-586-9110

Gary Epstein started Phoenix Artists in 1986 and merged with Los Angeles agent, Craig Wyckoff in 1991, giving both Epstein and Wyckoff visibility and offices for clients on both coasts.

Gary was still an actor when he began answering phones for his agent, Mort Schwartz, and unexpectedly began what was to become a career as an agent. Today Gary represents not only actors, but writers and directors as well.

Gary's nine year association with the prestigious Hesseltine Baker Agency gave him rigorous training for helming his own agency. E-W sees clients mostly by referral, but checks pictures and resumes.

Gary's associate, Mark Fleischman (Joan Scott, Curtis Brown) was a performer, casting director and manager before becoming an agent. Randi Ross (Don Buchwald & Associates and J. Michael Bloom) shepherds young adults and George Mastrogiorgis helms the literary department.

Agents
Gary Epstein, Mark Fleischman and Randi Ross
Client List
less than 100
Clients
Check Screen Actors Guild listings

✦ FBI/Frontier Booking International, Inc.

1560 Broadway, #1110
at 46th Street
New York, NY 10036
212-221-0220

Frontier Booking is not only one of the largest rock agencies around (they handle Sting, Snoop Doggy Dog, Modern English, Jane's Addiction and others), but they have a happening theatrical department as well. Ian Copeland started Frontier in 1979 for music clients and branched out into film, television and commercials in 1984.

John Shea (SEM&M and Kronick, Kelly & Lauren) heads up the theatrical department representing a hot list of young actors. Some from that list are Sean Nelson (*Fresh, American Buffalo*), Tracy Douglas (*Hallelujah, Concrete and Tinsel*), James Fall (*Pocahontas*), Courtney Chase (*Soul Man*), Jacqueline Torres (*FX*), Jessica Grant (*Dreams May Come*) and Jake Patellis,

Helping John run herd on this talented bunch are Justin Brown (who worked with Turtleback Productions) and Karen Apicella (Carson-Adler Agency).

FBI handles all types for all areas. They work with an extensive freelance list as well as with signed clients.

Agents
John Shea, Karen Apicella and Justin Brown
Client List
40 + freelance
Clients
Sean Nelson, Jake Patellis, Courtney Chase, James Fall, Jacqueline Torres, Jessica Grant, Tracy Douglas and others

---

✦ The Gage Group

315 W 57th Street
W of 8th Avenue
New York, NY 10036
212-541-5250

One of the most effective and respected agencies in town is owned by Martin Gage. Originally an actor, Martin was hit by a cab returning from his third callback for the role of Baby John in *West Side Story*. Whether Martin took this as a comment on his acting, I don't know, but when I met him, he was an agent with Fifi Oscard and for a while, they were partners.

The Gage Group has been a significant presence on the agency scene for many years now, and although Martin headquarters on the West Coast, he spends enough time in New York to really know all the clients.

The dynamic duo that run the New York office, Phil Adelman and Steve Unger are not only best friends, but their backgrounds and personalities are synergistic.

Theatre major, Steven Unger, taught high school after graduation while he was pondering what interesting direction his background might take him. When he found The Gage Group, he knew he was home. Phil Adelman is the ultimate hyphenate: screenwriter-elementary school teacher-director-musical director-composer-lyricist-quiz show writer. I can't think of anything Steve and Phil wouldn't be able to handle.

Pete Kaiser started working at The Gage Group as a bookkeeper for his day job when he was still an actor. He found the work so interesting that when a full-time job opened up, he asked to be part of the Group and is now the agent responsible for industrials and soaps. Wendie Relkin Adelman heads the commercial department.

When you see Phil's quotes elsewhere in this

book, you will get an idea of how this office operates, but for starters, Phil told me he would never think of releasing a client just because he wasn't getting work: *When a client of mine doesn't get work, I just figure the people who are doing the hiring are morons. I know when I take on a client that it's for life. I have so much faith in my own taste that I would never lose faith in a client.*

Agents
Phil Adelman, Steve Unger, Martin Gage and Pete Kaiser
Client List
65
Clients
Paul Benedict, Walter Charles, Marilyn Cooper, K Callan, Jane Connell, Dee Hoty, Gavin MacLeod, Debra Monk, Stephen Pearlman, John Cunningham, Marcia Lewis, Walter Bobbie, Liz Callaway, Nancy Ringham, Christine Andreas, Ernie Sabella, Edward Hibbert, B. J. Crosby and others

✦ Garber Talent Agency

2 Pennsylvania Plaza, #1910
7th Avenue between 32nd & 33rd Streets
New York, NY 10121
212-292-4910

Karen Garber was still in school studying theatre and communications when she got a job as a receptionist with the now defunct Joel Pitts Agency. She left Joel two years later to become an agent with Honey Sanders where she worked for 16 years.

In 1995, Karen decided to turn her fortunes in another direction, quit her job with Honey and accepted a job offer in another field. But, before she even started the job, she missed agenting, so she changed her plans and set about opening her own agency.

Well-connected in the casting community, Karen hit the ground running and is able to say that of her 46 clients, at least 90% are currently employed.

Clients include John Minco (*Chicago*), Michael Kubala (*Chicago*), Elena Ferrante (International company of *West Side Story*) and Birdie Hale (*Blind Faith*). Karen is particularly known for her strong list of dancers and choreographers.

This office works with signed clients theatrically, but does freelance for industrials and commercials. Although she does look at pictures and resumes, to get a call from Karen, you will need a strong resume.

Agents
Karen Garber
Client List
46
Clients
John Minco, Michael Kubala, Elena Ferrante, Birdie Hale and others

✦ The Gersh Agency New York

130 W 42nd Street, #2400
btwn 5th & 6th Avenues
New York, NY 10036
212-997-1818

The Gersh Agency New York was formed when Scott Yoselow, David Guc, Ellen Curren and Mary Meagher decided to leave Don Buchwald & Associates to form a New York office for the legendary Phil Gersh.

Scott Yoselow is the sole remaining founding partner, but he has staffed GANY with effective agents with valuable backgrounds. Victoria Johnson (Susan Smith) was in theatre production and Lindsay Porter and Sally Tannenbaum were both casting executives. William Butler (WMA), Larry Taube (WMA) and Stephen Hirsh (Paradigm) are all graduates of their former employers' agency training programs.

This agency prefers well-trained actors and is meticulous about monitoring new talent by attending showcases and readings. If you don't have a referral, concentrate on doing remarkable work in a showcase and ask them to come and see it.

The client list shared by The Gersh Agency on both coasts is outstanding. Here are some of their impressive clients: Fran Drescher, David Schwimmer, Calista Flockhart, Jane Krakowski, Barry Bostwick, Roma Downey, Patsy Kensit, Shirley Knight, Lea Thompson, Dan Butler, Jeffrey DeMunn, Victor Garber, Dan Hedaya, Eriq LaSalle, Christopher Lloyd, Esai Morales, Robert Prosky, Michael Rooker, John Glover, Dan Futterman and Kyle Secor.

The Gersh Agency New York continues the top level representation Phil Gersh pioneered for actors, writers, directors, authors and below-the-line clients.

Agents

Scott Yoselow, Victoria Johnson, Lindsay Porter, William Butler, Sally Tannenbaum, Larry Taube and Stephen Hirsh

Client List

220 (NY/LA)

Clients

David Schwimmer, Calista Flockhart, Jane Krakowski, Barry Bostwick, Roma Downey, Fran Drescher, Patsy Kensit, Shirley Knight, Lea Thompson, Dan Butler, Jeffrey DeMunn, Dan Futterman, Victor Garber, John Glover, Dan Hedaya, Eriq LaSalle, Christopher Lloyd, Esai Morales, Robert Prosky, Michael Rooker, Kyle Secor and others

✦ The Gilchrist Talent Group

630 9th Avenue, 8th floor
between 44th and 45th Streets
New York, NY 10036
212-692-9166

Pat Gilchrist first became known as the mom of *Mikey*, the adorable kid from the Life cereal commercials. The Gilchrists had seven other appealing Mikeys at home and since they were all working in commercials, Pat decided to start her own agency.

In addition to her adventures shepherding her own kids to auditions, she learned about agenting by apprenticing at Rascals Unlimited and with the encouragement of her husband, Tom Gilchrist (an ex-cop), started her own business in 1982.

Today, Gilchrist is known as the *Professional Mom/Agent* to some of film and television's most visible teen and child stars.

Gilchrist also books children and teens for commercials.

GTG is constantly on the lookout for new kids and religiously looks at all pictures and resumes. No clients over age 25.

Agents
Pat Gilchrist
Client List
45-55
Clients
Check Screen Actors Guild listings

✦ Peggy Hadley Enterprises, Ltd.

250 W 57th Street
btwn 7th & 8th Avenues
New York, NY 10107
212-246-2166

Another actor who changed sides of the desk, Peggy Hadley has never missed performing. When she was searching for a new career, fellow performer Fannie Flagg talked Peggy into becoming her manager. Peggy managed Fannie and four others until their careers drew them West. Peggy (a transplanted Kentuckian) felt she couldn't bear leaving the city to go with them to Los Angeles, so she just added more actors to her list and became an agent.

She has about 60-70 signed clients and works with many others freelance. She handles only legit, no commercials..

When I asked Peggy for clients' names, she said she didn't want to name any lest she leave someone out, so, as I usually do, I chose a couple of names from her list.

Agents
Peggy Hadley
Client List
60-70
Clients
Lou Myers, Beth Fowler and others

✦ HWA Talent Representatives

36 E 22nd Street, 3rd Floor
btwn Park Avenue S & Broadway
New York, NY 10010
212-889-0800

Barbara Harter and Patty Woo paid their dues at
a succession of instructive and successful venues before
teaming to produce this thriving agency. Patty, who heads
the Los Angeles office began in the business as an
assistant for Monty Silver before becoming his colleague
and ultimately partnering with Robby Kass (Kass Woo).

Barbara was a casting director (*The Guiding Light*
and Jane Iredale Associates) before J. Michael Bloom
drafted her to head up the model portion of his business.

Since opening her first agency in 1986 (Barbara
Harter & Associates), Barbara has partnered with Ellen
Manning in Harter Manning and combined with both
Woo and Manning at Harter Manning Woo. The partner-
ship is down to two again since Manning has left the
business.

Harter Woo presides over a large combined Los
Angeles/New York list of about 300 signed clients.
Among the many working actors on their list are James
Gandolfini (*Angie, Crimson Tide*), Saundra Quarterman
(*Hangin' with Mr. Cooper*) Tom Amandes (*Pursuit of
Happiness*), Lucky Vanous and Frederique van der Wal.

Harter heads the modeling area of the business
and handles celebrities and contracts. The theatrical
department is led by Diana Doussant (APA) with help
from colleagues Mary Collins (J. Michael Bloom), Alan
Willig, Jay Kane, David McDermott, Annette Paperella
and Bill Ionone (Ionone-Day, Judy Schoen Agency).

HWA has grown in strength theatrically and still
maintains its edge in the commercial and modeling areas
of the business.

Agents

Diana Doussant, Bill Ionone, Mary Collins, Alan Willig,
Jay Kane, David McDermott and Annette Paperella

Client List

300 combined coasts

Clients

James Gandolfini, Saundra Quarterman, Lucky Vanous,
Frederique van der Wal, Tom Amandes and others

✦ Harden-Curtis Associates

850 7th Avenue, #405
btwn 55th & 56th Streets
New York, NY 10019
212-977-8502

Mary Harden and Nancy Curtis are now partners, but in 1981, when Mary was partnered by Bret Adams, one of many inspired things Mary did at that office was to hire Nancy.

Fifteen years later (1996) Mary and Nancy opened their own agency representing actors and writers. Mary heads their important literary division while Nancy leads the acting clients.

Nancy studied acting for 7 years as a child, but her parents felt she should pursue a *real job*, so she ended up with a Masters Degree in advertising from Michigan State University. She worked at Leo Burnett in Chicago and at Ted Bates in New York before a wise colleague suggested since Nancy was more addicted to reading plays than *Advertising Age*, that perhaps her interests lay elsewhere.

It didn't take Nancy long to land a job as Bret Adams' assistant and then to move up to agenting. Since marketing is such a necessary element in an actor's career, her advertising background has been invaluable.

Nancy's advice to all clients is to *Run your own company!* and is, in fact, what she envisions on her tombstone.

Harden-Curtis' list of 60 signed clients includes Tony winner, Ruben Santiago-Hudson (*Michael Hayes*), *Linda Emond (*Nine Armenians, 1776, Baby Anger*), Kathryn Hays (*As the World Turns*), Sherri Alexander (*As the World Turns*), Peter Hermann (*The Guiding Light*), *Mary Lou Rosato (*Once Upon a Mattress*), Dennis Kelly (*Damn Yankees*) and David Margulies. This office works with freelance talent only as a prelude to signing.

Colleague Yvonne Kenney is also an Adams alumnae. Robert Kohn and Diane Riley assist Harden and Curtis.

This office represents actors and writers and sees new clients mainly through referral.

Agents
Nancy Curtis, Mary Harden and Yvonne Kenney
Client List
60
Clients
David Margulies, Ruben Santiago-Hudson, *Mary Lou Rosato, *Linda Emond, Kathryn Hays, Sherri Alexander, Peter Hermann, Dennis Kelly and others

*Shared clients with Susan Smith

✦ Henderson-Hogan Agency Inc.

850 7th Avenue, #1003
btwn 56th & 57th Streets
New York, NY 10019
212-765-5190

An actor who decided against the instability of the actor's life, Jerry Hogan worked as a private secretary to actress Margaret Leighton before his first job in the agency business at The Dudley, Field & Malone Agency. He was a commercial agent at United Talent before joining Maggie Henderson years ago.

Robert Frye (Richard Astor), Mark Upchurch (J. Michael Bloom) and George Lutsch (who trained at H/H) join Jerry in representing clients like David Groh, Kathleen Freeman, Edward Albert, Earle Hyman, Kim Hamilton, Dakin Matthews (*Soul Man*) and Brad Sullivan (*Nothing Sacred*). Jean Walton heads up the children's division.

Although H/H prefers to work with signed clients, they do occasionally freelance with former clients and/or old friends.

Maggie Henderson died recently and although Jerry ran the east coast office and Maggie was always on the west coast, her passing is a terrible loss to everyone.

Agents
Jerry Hogan, Mark Upchurch, George Lutsch, Jean Walton and Robert Frye
Client List
60 +
Clients
Earle Hyman, David Groh, Anne Francis, Kathleen Freeman, Kim Hamilton, Edward Albert, Dakin Matthews, Brad Sullivan and others

✦ Ingber & Associates

274 Madison Avenue
btwn 39th & 40th Streets
New York, NY 10016
212-889-9450

Carole Ingber worked in motion picture advertising before moving to Los Angeles to work in casting
with Vicki Rosenberg in 1982. Since returning from the
west coast, she has worked at a succession of high profile
commercial talent agencies: J. Michael Bloom, SEM&M
and LW2. For a while she ran the commercial arm of
Susan Smith's distinguished agency; all this in preparation
for opening her own office in 1993.

Although I&A is a commercial agency, I include
them because they specialize in handling the commercial
careers of working actors. If you are already working
good jobs as an actor and are looking for someone to
handle the commercial part of your business, Carole
Ingber may be the woman to talk to.

This agency also handles a few industrials and
print for their clients.

Agents
Carole R. Ingber
Client List
160 + freelance
Clients
Working actors

✦ Innovative Artists

1776 Broadway, #1810
at 45th Street
New York, NY 10019
212-315-4455

Gersh alums Howard Goldberg and Scott Harris opened the New York edition of their prestigious Los Angeles agency, Harris and Goldberg in 1991.

Harris helms the Los Angeles office while another Gersh alum, David Guc (pronounced Gus) is in charge in New York. Guc started in the business at Susan Smith and worked for Don Buchwald before starting The Gersh Agency in New York. Claudia Black (Paradigm) and Gary Gersh (no relation) who became an agent through the agent-training-program at Innovative and Richie Jackson who was Harvey Fierstein's assistant, all join David in representing a list of distinguished clients.

Clients include Tatum O'Neal, Michael Rapaport, Molly Ringwald, Faith Prince, Ralph Waite, Raquel Welsh, Lou Diamond Phillips, Estelle Getty, Martin Sheen, Peter Ustinov and Harvey Fierstein.

This agency is high on casting directors' lists because Innovative's experience and aggressiveness have attracted an impressive list of clients.

Agents
David Guc, Gary Gersh, Richie Jackson and Claudia Black
Client List
75
Clients
Molly Ringwald, Lou Diamond Phillips, Harvey Fierstein, Faith Prince, Ralph Waite, Raquel Welch, Estelle Getty, Martin Sheen, Peter Ustinov, Tatum O'Neal, Michael Rapaport and others

✦ ICM/International Creative Management

40 W 57th Street
just W of 5th Avenue
New York, NY 10019
212-556-5600

Though ICM was already in contention for the
title of #1 well before CAA's founding fathers left the
agency business for new challenges, the restructuring
allowed some loyal CAA clients to finally consider
another agency. ICM was waiting and gained an even
larger share of A list actors, writers, directors, producers,
musical artists, authors, newscasters and sports figures.

Known to be less corporate than WMA and
CAA (that means everyone in the corporation doesn't
have to be called in to review your latest contract), ICM
is described by insiders as a stylish, forward thinking
operation. Headed by president Jim Wiatts, dynamic ICM
is intent dominating the conglomerate agency scene.

Formed when Ashley-Famous and CMA merged
in 1971, this agency has many, many clients and many,
many agents. The most famous are powerful Sam Cohn
who heads the New York office and Los Angeles'
charismatic Ed Limato. Limato was profiled in a *Vanity
Fair* article, *The Famous Eddie L* in January 1990.

Close on the heels of Cohn and Limato are two
powerful emerging female agents:

✦   *In motion picture talent, a major factor [in the rise of
ICM's fortunes] is the presence of senior VP Elaine Goldsmith-
Thomas, who represents Julia Roberts, Spike Lee and Tim
Robbins, and who is arguably one of the most powerful female
agents in the biz.*

*ICM's Gotham office is also home to agent Aleen
Keshishian, who has helped nurture numerous young actors into
stars, including Natalie Portman, Skeet Ulrich and Edward*

Norton.

> *Agents Go Gotham*
> Diane Goldner
> *Daily Variety*
> August 29, 1997

No matter who your responsible agent is, it's clear that ICM would be a happy choice for anyone with the credits and/or heat to compete with their stable of luminous clients.

Agents
Sam Cohn, Elaine Goldsmith-Thomas, Bart Walker, Bridget Aschenberg, Boaty Boatwright, Arlene Donovan, Andrea Eastman, Aleen Keshishian, Sue Leibman, Sarah Jane Leigh, Pearl Martino, Todd Noonan and others

Client List
Very large

Clients
James Woods, Julia Roberts, Kim Basinger, Judy Davis, Tim Robbins, Susan Sarandon, Michelle Pfeiffer, Denzel Washington, Stephen Rea, Joan Plowright, Mike Nichols, Vanessa Redgrave, Ralph Bakshi, Natalie Portman, Spike Lee, Skeet Ulrich, Rene Balcer, Peter P. Benchley, Garry Marshall and many, many others

✦ Integrity Talent

165 W 46ᵗʰ Street, #1210
btwn 6ᵗʰ & 7ᵗʰ Avenues
New York, NY 10036
212-575-5756

Wendy Wetstein has always known how to get what she wants. When she was 15 years old she was bitten by the show biz bug at a performance of *Cats*. Determined to become a part of this world, she pretended to work for her school newspaper and asked for an interview with dancer, Timothy Scott. She interviewed Scott and became friends not only with Scott, but with most of the cast, musicians and crew.

Having experienced Wendy's resourcefulness and drive, Scott advised Wetstein (by then a high school senior) that she should be an agent. When he explained that agents helped actors get jobs and that he wanted her to be his agent when she made it, Wendy's course was set.

She attended Fordham University — The College at Lincoln Center, taking courses in media, journalism, theatre and television while interning in both casting (Binder Casting) and theatrical agencies (Select Artists, Abrams Artists).

One of twenty-eight students chosen from 600 by the Academy of Television Arts and Sciences to intern for a Summer in Los Angeles, Wendy's plum assignment was in business affairs at Writers & Artists, listening daily to important negotiations.

Homesick for Broadway, Wendy returned to the Big Apple to work at Ambrosio/Mortimer for Mark Schlegel (now at J. Michael Bloom), as a publicist for political satirist, Mort Sahl and in talent payment at Grey Advertising. In the Fall of 1993, Wetstein returned to agenting where she was franchised by Barry Haft Brown.

By June of 1995, Wendy was finally prepared to do things her way and opened her own office. Judy Malloy (*Side Show*), Larry Linville *(M*A*S*H)*, Craig Schulman (*Les Miserables, The Phantom of the Opera*), Gerry Vichi (*How to Succeed in Business Without Really Trying*), Don Johanson (*Cats, Jelly's Last Jam*), Christian Nova, Rachel Lynn Ricca and Michael Visconti are representative of her 80 signed clients. This office does not work with freelance talent.

The pivotal *Cats* performance has produced a formidable presence on the agency scene. Wendy's background, vitality and imagination continue to move her clients forward.

Agents
Wendy Wetstein
Client List
80
Clients
Judy Malloy, Larry Linville, Craig Schulman, Gerry Vichi, Mamie Duncan-Gibbs, Don Johanson, Christian Nova, Rachel Lynn Ricca, Michael Visconti and others

✦ Jan J. Agency, Inc.

365 W 34th Street
btwn 7th & 8th Avenues
New York, NY 10001
212-967-5265

A child actor who majored in communications in college, Jan Jarrett was a little ahead of her time when she tried to enter the male-dominated newscaster market in 1970. Deciding that she was *not that big a trailblazer,* Jan (who had watched her mother manage actors) opened her own children's talent agency. A real family endeavor, when Jan left to raise children, her father ran the business until she returned in 1980.

Although the agency has represented adults periodically, their focus today is children only. As a child or teenage client ages, Jan continues to represent them, but takes no new clients over 20.

Jan works with 40-50 signed clients for theatre, film, television and commercials. She also handles freelancers. As with most agents, signed clients are the #1 priority.

Colleague Mayce (pronounced Macy) Nierenberg is from South Jersey. She was drawn to show biz and entered it by begging her friend's mom for a job. That mom was Cathy Parker, who ran her own management company. She gave Mayce a job as her assistant. Mayce learned the agent side of the business by assisting at Abrams Artists before joining Jan representing clients like Adam Zolotin (*Jack, Leave It to Beaver*), Joanna Pacitti (*Broadway Kids*), Peter Dunn (*A Christmas Carol*), Blake Bashoff (*Swiss Family Robinson, Bushwhacked, Big Bully*), Patrick Levis (*Big*) and Matt Carey (*Creature*).

Agents
Jan Jarrett and Mayce Nierenberg
Client List
50-60 + freelance
Clients
Adam Zolotin, Blake Bashoff, Matt Carey, Patrick Levis, Peter Dunn, Joanna Pacitti and others

✦ Jordon Gill & Dornbaum Agency, Inc.

156 5th Avenue, #711
at 20th Street
New York, NY
212-463-8455

Robin Dornbaum and Jeffrey Gill, owners of this hot 30-year-old agency specializing in children, were both under 30 when they bought the agency in 1988.

Although Robin loved actors and wanted to *work with them in some way,* she never knew how until as a communications major, she spent six months interning with the legendary Marje Fields. Robin knew quickly she had found her calling. After six months, mentor Fields sent her to work in casting at Reed Sweeney Reed, where she worked for free, honing her skills, storing information and growing in the business.

When she graduated from school and casting six months later, Sweeney introduced her to the Joe Jordon Agency. Originally an agency for adults, Jordon's son, Vance (now a famous art gallery owner), focused the agency onto the lucrative children's marketplace.

Vance hired a prominent children's agent and Robin became her assistant. When the agent left two years later, Vance had to decide between selling the agency or revitalizing it in some way. He opted for a new management team promoting Robin to agent and luring child-agent-specialist, Jeffrey Gill (Bonni Kidd, Fifi Oscard) to be her partner. Robin and Jeff were both young (24), savvy and industrious. Their hard work changed the agency into one of the top kid agencies in New York.

Jeff and Robin head the commercial department with Jenny Carbone (Terrific Talent) and Jana Kogan-Barth (J. Michael Bloom) representing kids for film, theatre and television. They have 60-70 signed clients and work extensively with managers.

Prospective clients should send in snapshots, not professional pictures. Clients include Julia Weldon (*Before and After*), Justin Restivo (*Leave it to Beaver*), Charlie Hofheimer (*Lassie, Boys, On the Waterfront*), Amy Hargraves (*Matt Waters, Flashback*), Emily Mae Young, (*Step by Step*), Michael Angarano (*For Richer or Poorer*), Terry Butler (*Beauty and the Beast*), Evan Newman (*Les Miserables, The Capeman*) and Huckleberry Fox (*Crazy for a Kiss*).

Agents
Jenny Carbone and Jana Kogan-Barth
Client List
50-60
Clients
Julia Weldon, Charlie Hofheimer, Aaron Schwartz, Huckleberry Fox, Amy Hargraves, Michael Angarano, Emily Mae Young, Justin Restivo, Terry Butler, Evan Newman and others

✦ Jerry Kahn, Inc.

853 7th Avenue
btwn 53rd & 54th Streets
New York, NY 10036
212-245-7317

In 1958, Jerry Kahn left his job as a press agent to join Louis Maxwell Rosen and represent the likes of Dustin Hoffman and Ron Leibman. He also worked with William Schuller before opening his own office in 1968. Theatre, film, and television are the main thrusts of the agency although Jerry has been known to book an occasional commercial.

An old-fashioned agent who is happy to rep a small list and do it with care and integrity, Jerry didn't know what I was talking about when I asked what his biggest complaint about actors would be. Now, that's nice.

Agents
Jerry Kahn
Client List
20-25
Clients
Barbara Montgomery, Karen Lynn Gorney and others

✦ Kerin - Goldberg Associates

155 E 55th Street, # 5D
btwn 3rd & Lexington Avenues
New York, NY 10022
212-838-7373

Charles Kerin's interest in the business was so strong that in his first job as a publicist for Scholastic Magazine, he managed to convince management to create a film award just so he could get to see free movies. That same kind of creative thinking led Charles to a job with prestigious old-line office, Coleman-Rosenberg where he became an agent. Charles left C-R to open his own literary agency representing soap writers in 1985.

Partner, Ellie Goldberg was an actress when old school chum, Gary Epstein cajoled her into joining his office and becoming an agent. Goldberg's path has also included stints with Henderson-Hogan, Bonni Allen and ultimately, Coleman-Rosenberg. Although Charles was working at another agency, when he was called on to broker a literary deal for one of C-R's theatrical clients, he and Ellie hit it off immediately and spoke often of opening their own agency *when the time is right*.

1995 turned out to be the magic year when Kerin and Goldberg got together to create this classy agency representing actors, playwrights, directors, composers, choreographers, songwriters, scene designers, costume designers and art directors.

Ellie, Charles and associate Ron Ross (Waters Nicolosi) represent the prestigious list of big name and working actors who grace the client list at this thriving agency. They see new clients only by referral but do look at all pictures and resumes.

There are incisive quotes from Ellie elsewhere in the book. Be sure to check them out.

Agents
Charles Kerin, Ellie Goldberg and Ron Ross
Client List
100
Clients
Check Screen Actors Guild listings

✦ The Krasny Office, Inc.

1501 Broadway, #1303
at 43rd Street
New York, NY 10019
212-730-8160

Gary Krasny has a valuable background for an agent. He was an actor, a publicist for Berkeley Books, a story editor for Craig Anderson (after he left the Hudson Theatre Guild) and worked as an assistant to Broadway General Manager, Norman Rothstein at Theatre Now. In 1985, he decided he was more empathetic with the artist than management and decided to become an agent.

Gary honed his agenting skills at various agencies before opening his own in late 1991. He found office space not only in the same building, but on the same floor where he had worked with Craig Anderson many years before.

Gary's background, experience and taste have made him a favorite with the casting community, so when he opened his office, he quickly became part of the mainstream.

Norma Eisenbaum (Sharon Ambrose) and Mary Haggerty (Ann Wright) run the highly successful commercial, voice over and print department. B. Lynne Jebens (Michael Hartig) and Fleurette Vincent (who went from intern to assistant to agent at this agency) are Gary's colleagues in the legit department.

The Krasny Office continues to thrive and grow. Clients from their list include Carl Gordon, Alan Feinstein, David Bailey, Brad English, Patricia Medina and Meg Mundy. The Krasny Office has liaison arrangements with several Los Angeles agents and managers.

Agents
Gary Krasny, B. Lynne Jebens and Fleurette Vincent
Client List
85
Clients
Carl Gordon, Alan Feinstein, David Bailey, Brad English, Patricia Medina, Meg Mundy and others

✦ LTA/Lally Talent Agency

Film Center Building
630 9th Avenue, #800
at 44th Street
New York, NY 10036
212-974-8718

Dale Lally was an actor and a personal manager before he crossed the desk to became an agent. He worked for Mary Ellen White and Nobel Talent prior to becoming partners with print agents, Wallace Rogers and Peter Lerman (Lally Rogers & Lerman). Lally, Rogers and Lerman decided to go their separate ways and Lally opened his own office in June of 1992.

Stephen Laviska was a contract lawyer before he joined Dale representing their strong list of musical performers, interesting young adults and solid character people. Actors from their list include Tom Flagg, James Lally (no relation), Angel Caban, Timothy Warmen, Jerome Preston Bates, Jodie Langel, Brenda Denmark, Rob Evan, Kansas Rose and Bradley Glenn.

Agents
Dale Lally and Stephen Laviska
Client List
45
Clients
Tom Flagg, James Lally, Angel Caban, Timothy Warmen, Jerome Preston Bates, Jodie Langel, Brenda Denmark, Rob Evan, Kansas Rose, Bradley Glenn and others

✦ The Lantz Office

888 7th Avenue, #3001
btwn 56th & 57th Streets
New York, NY 10106
212-586-0200

When I quizzed New York agents as to other agents they admired, Robert Lantz was the name most mentioned. One of the class acts in the annals of show-biz, Lantz started in the business as a story editor. On a Los Angeles business trip from his London home in 1950, Phil Berg, of the famous Berg-Allenbery Agency, made him an offer he couldn't refuse: *Don't go home. Come to New York. Open a New York office for us.* Mr. Lantz opened their New York office at 3 East 57th Street and represented Clark Gable, Madeleine Carroll and other illustrious stars until William Morris bought that company a year later.

Lantz worked for smaller agencies for a few years before opening Robert Lantz, Ltd. in 1954. In 1955, he succumbed to Joe Mankiewicz's pleas to join his efforts producing films. It took three years for Lantz to figure out that he found agenting a much more interesting profession.

In 1958, Lantz reentered the field as a literary agent. Feeling that a mix of actors and directors and writers gave each segment more power, his list soon reflected that.

Dennis Aspland worked for the legendary Sam Cohn before joining The Lantz Office to represent screenwriters, directors and actors. The main thrust of the agency continues to be writers and directors, but they do represent a few high-end actors.

Agents
Robert Lantz and Dennis Aspland
Client List
20
Clients
Liv Ullman, Polly Holiday and others

✦ Leudeke Agency

630 9th Avenue, 8th floor
between 44th & 45th Streets
New York, NY 10036
212-765-9564

Penny Leudeke is such an entrepreneur that at
the age of 12, she had a small business. When she design-
ed and made a bag for her violinist-mother's neck rest,
other violinists saw the bag and became customers.

Trained as an opera singer, Penny's energy could
not be harnessed just for herself. In addition to design-
ing and making gowns for an opera company, she found
herself always getting jobs for her friends.

When Penny determined that she loved agenting
more than singing, but would like to get paid for it, she
approached children's agent, Pat Gilchrist about starting
an adult department at her agency.

Penny shared space with Gilchrist for a year
before opening her office in August of 1997. Her list is
eclectic. In addition to representing actors like ex-pro
football player, Jariod Bunch (*Only in America: the Life and
Crimes of Don King*), David Roya (the bad guy in the *Billy
Jack* movies), opera singer-actor Robert McKenzie
(*Christmas Carol, The Long Kiss Goodnight*) and Howard
Wilkerson (*Smokey Joe's, Creature*). Penny also lists
premiere American baritone, Sherrill Milnes, legendary
jazz sax players James Moody and Kenny Barrett,
classical composer, Anthony Davis who wrote the music
for *Angels in America* and various writers, dancers and
singers as part of her professional family.

Penny looks carefully at all pictures and resumes
and has found a couple of her most successful clients that
way. Penny's colleague is Teresa Wolf (The Sanders
Agency Ltd.).

Agent
Penny Leudeke and Teresa Wolf
Client List
50
Clients
Jariod Bunch, David Roya, Robert McKenzie,
Howard Wilkerson and others

◆ Lionel Larner, Ltd.

119 W 54th Street, #1412
btwn 6th & 7th Avenues
New York, NY 10019
212-246-3105

Lionel Larner is one of the classiest agents in town both in demeanor and client list. His first job in the business was as European casting director for Otto Preminger on the film, *St. Joan.* When he turned in his casting hat for that of an agent, he was trained by the CAA's legendary Martin Baum while they were both at GAC. In 1969, when Lionel left Baum and GAC (now ICM), he started Lionel Larner, Ltd.

Not only did Lionel start at the top, he has remained there with prestigious clients like Glenda Jackson, Carroll O'Connor, Madeleine Potter, Diana Rigg, Simon MacCorkindale and Stacy Keach.

LL, Ltd. is not strictly a star agency, Lionel represents actors on every level.

Lionel admits to being a real snob about his clients, demanding they have impeccable theatre backgrounds. Well, why not? *He* does. One of the perks of this book has been meeting people like Lionel who return phone calls, are responsible, creative, caring and have taste, style, stature, and access.

Agents
Lionel Larner
Client List
40
Clients
Carroll O'Connor, Glenda Jackson, Stacy Keach, Madeleine Potter, Diana Rigg, Simon MacCorkindale and others

✦ Bruce Levy Agency

335 W 38th Street, #802
btwn 8th & 9th Avenues
New York, NY 10018
212-563-7079

Life is an adventure should be emblazoned on the
forehead of Bruce Levy. An actor, a producer (*The Price of
Genius*) and an entrepreneur who can do anything, Bruce
Levy finally decided to put all those talents together and
open an agency. On opening day, October 2, 1992, Bruce
found himself up to his ears in work and in actors.

A man who doesn't know how to do things
halfway, Bruce gives the kind of attention that has
attracted actors with important resumes. Motivated actors
inspire him to even greater heights.

The office includes a well-equipped theatre in
which to view clients and would-be clients. Bruce is
interested in making money for himself and his clients,
but his quest is for quality. Actors with the same mind set
will find a happy and rewarding relationship with the
Bruce Levy Agency.

Since the last edition of this book, Bruce and
many of his freelance clients have gotten married so his
list is now comprised mostly of signed clients with a few
freelancers in an engagement period. Two from his list
are Sylvia Miles and Mark Baker.

Agents
Bruce Levy
Client List
30
Clients
Sylvia Miles, Mark Baker and others

✦ McDonald Richards Inc.

56 5th Avenue
at 20th Street
New York, NY 10010
212-627-3100

In 1983 actor/model Arthur Bronfin and model/actor Scott McDonald decided to join forces to open an agency representing actors and models for commercial print work. Sadly, Scott died in 1988 before seeing the incredible success the agency has become. McDonald Richards is now the largest commercial print house in New York with 5 agents handling the huge list of freelance actors working through this agency.

Although the emphasis here is definitely on commercial print *for actors from birth to death in every ethnic category,* McDonald Richards does occasionally book actors for film and television, so a picture and resume sent here could result in a print job and/or a theatrical booking.

In addition to Arthur, agents in this office are Joan Stephens, Gary Bertalovitz, Tricia La Bracio and Maureen Larkin. This office also books models with disabilities.

In case you are wondering (as was my editor) where *Richards* comes from in this agency's name, that is Arthur's middle name.

Agents
Arthur Bronfin, Joan Stephens, Gary Bertalovitz, Tricia La Bracio and Maureen Larkin
Client List
Freelance
Clients
Freelance

✦ Nouvelle Talent, Inc.

453 W 17th Street, 3rd floor
btwn 9th & 10th Avenues
New York, NY 10011
212-645-0940

Toni Sipka was working in Chicago as a spokes-
person and narrator at trade shows and doing corporate
promotion when she decided to open her own agency
and book others into the same kinds of jobs.

She opened her first office in Chicago in 1987
and quickly spawned satellites in New York and Las
Vegas. Until 1997, the New York office was run by
associate, B. G. Gross, but at that time, Ann decided to
moved to New York and run this office herself.

Known professionally for a few years by her
married name, Ann Bordalo, Toni has made the decision
to return to her maiden name, Toni (Antoinette) Sipka.
Although she says she will answer to either, she wants to
reestablish her old identity, so it's Toni now, instead of
Ann.

Toni says actors are naturals at spokespersons
and narrators and she happily helps them in making the
transition to that area of the business. She does call talent
from pictures and resumes. Pictures that catch her eye
feature a nice smile, are clean, crisp, warm, neat and
professional.

In women Toni looks for a sexy wholesomeness
instead of the fresh-scrubbed look. She seeks men with a
well-groomed look and likes a ¾ length shot.

Performers who sing and dance are a valuable
commodity for corporate promotion, so be sure to list
your other attributes. Toni also gets calls for cruise ship
performers.

Toni is one agent who likes to be called weekly
and quizzed as to *What's going on.* She says that when

talent calls her, she knows they are interested in working. If they don't call, she tends to forget about them.

Toni is joined by colleague John Protomaster. John was in marketing before he became part of the Nouvelle family.

If you have interest in this area, Nouvelle sounds like an exceptional resource.

Agents

Toni Sipka and John Protomaster

Client List

Large

Clients

Freelance

✦ Omnipop

55 West Old Country Road
Hicksville, NY 11801
516-937-6011

Though I couldn't have imagined Long Island as a spawning ground for an influential show-biz agency, Omnipop has managed to spawn and then some. Tom Ingegno (engine-yo), Ralph Asquino and Bruce Smith started this agency on Long Island in 1983 and from the beginning, they prospered.

An eclectic lot, the Omni partners are all stand-up performers, musicians or managers who booked themselves and their friends on college circuits and later clubs. As they graduated to bigger, more diverse venues and clients, starting an agency was a logical progression. Omnipop consciously chooses staff that share this background.

Their taste and savvy led them to create their own niche representing stand-up comics for personal appearances, television, film and commercials.

In their one concession to tradition, Bruce Smith moved to Los Angeles to open a West Coast head-quarters in 1990. Tom runs things on Long Island. He says that having an office out of Manhattan allows them to spend less time commuting and more time doing their work. Tom says they still come into The City: *We go out and scout a lot of people and develop them. We discover a lot of talent in New York because a lot of comedy comes from here.*

Omni books stand-up performers exclusively so don't bother sending pictures and resumes here unless this is your goal. Although the Los Angeles office is only interested if you have already spent at least a year in the business and are playing a decent venue, the East Coast office see themselves as *the farm team*, developing the stars of tomorrow, so they're a little more approachable. Still, you really should have 20-30 minutes worth of material before you query this agency.

Omni represents comedians who also act but, they don't sign actors as such. Their interest lies chiefly in comedians who have developed a clear persona for their material thus making them ripe for crossover engagements.

Clients routinely work *The Tonight Show, The Late Show with David Letterman, Late Night with Conan O'Brien* and *E! Entertainment,* as well as clubs, film and theatre.

There are some helpful insights from Bruce and Tom about career progression for stand-ups elsewhere in the book.

Clients from their list include Kathy Buckley, Andy Kindler, Christopher Titus, Ian Bagg and Greg Proops.

Contact this office before you send an audition tape. Best way to access these folk is via a phone call or letter stating who you are and what you've done. If they find you and/or your background interesting, they will either ask to see a tape or come see you work.

Agents
Tom Ingegno, Ralph Asquino, Joan St. Onge, Simon Hopkins and Barbara Klein
Client List
40 combined NY/LA list
Clients
Kathy Buckley, Andy Kindler, Christopher Titus, Ian Bagg, Greg Proops and others

✦ Oppenheim-Christie Ltd.

13 E 37th Street, 7th floor
just E of 5th Avenue
New York, NY 10016
212-213-4330

Oppenheim-Christie has long been known as an agency representing actors for commercials and voice overs but the merger with H. Shep Pamplin's Sheplin Artists extends the reach to include legit actors, writers, directors, dancers, comedians, singers and variety artists.

Initially an actor-director-producer-set designer, Pamplin's frustration at his inability to get agents and casting directors to attend showcases led to a suggestion from his agent, Bob Donaghey at Talent East that he might be more effective if he just became an agent.

Shep joined Bob as an agent and has never looked back. He opened his own office in 1994 and merged with Oppenheim-Christie in mid 1997.

Oppenheim-Christie continues to emphasize representation for actors for commercials while Shep works with a signed list of about 32 singers and 25 actors for film and television. Like most agents, in order to protect himself from spending time introducing an actor to the marketplace and having another agent reap the rewards of his work, Shep works with clients only briefly on a freelance basis solely as a prelude to signing.

Shep has some good comments elsewhere in the book that you might find interesting.

Agents
H. Shep Pamplin
Client List
57
Clients
Check Screen Actors Guild listings

✦ Fifi Oscard Agency, Inc.

24 W 40th Street
just W of 5th Avenue
New York, NY 10018
212-764-1100

Fifi Oscard was a frustrated housewife and
mother in 1949 when she began working gratis for Lee,
Harris, Draper. When I asked her in what capacity she
was working, she said, *mostly as a jerk* but added that in
nine months she was no longer inept and had worked
herself up to $15 a week. Always interested in theatre and
with the ability *to do almost anything*, Fifi has prospered.

Today she holds forth over a giant agency that
represents actors, directors, producers, composers,
singers, authors and playwrights in every area of entertainment and publishing. The agency handles about 200
signed clients for theatre, film and television, and services
freelance people mainly in the courtship stage before
signing them. Fifi continues to be the same warm, shrewd
Earth mother I encountered early in my career.

Carmen La Via heads the legit department with
help from fellow agents, Peter Sawyer, Francis Del Duca,
and John Medeiros. Graham Murray runs the commercial
and children's department. Actors may send photos and
resumes. Reels should only be presented on request.

Agents
Fifi Oscard, Carmen La Via, Peter Sawyer, John Medeiros
and Francis Del Duca
Client List
200
Clients
William Shatner, Ken Howard, George Plimpton,
Jean Marsh, Leon Redbone and others

✦ Harry Packwood Talent, Ltd.

250 W 57th Street, #2012
at Broadway
New York, NY 10107
212-586-8900

Once an actor on *The Patty Duke Show*, when Harry Packwood decided to become an agent, he went into business with his mother, Doris. The Packwoods run an efficient thriving office.

Doris and Harry see people mainly through referrals but do look at all pictures and resumes. They are interested in clients over the long haul and support them by being professional, energetic, caring and personable.

The office works extensively with freelance talent as well as having a signed list of about 25.

Agents
Harry Packwood and Doris Packwood
Client List
25 + freelance
Clients
Check Screen Actors Guild listings

✦ Dorothy Palmer Talent Agency, Inc.

235 W 56th Street, #24K
btwn 7th & 8th Avenues
New York, NY, 10019
212-765-4280

Dorothy Palmer Talent Agency has 14,000 names in its talent computer and 450 in its annual Palmer People Book. Dorothy has about a dozen signed clients.

One would think with all these faces and resumes that the proprietor here would be either out of her mind or totally unapproachable. Neither is true. Dorothy seems to not only have everything in hand but to be pretty calm and together about things. She trained with Sol Hurok Enterprises and worked with National Concert and Artists Corporation before starting her own agency in 1974.

Dorothy's list includes entertainers, actors, writers and producers, many of whom are hyphenates like singer-composer Nicole Paddington, actress-impersonator Holly Farris, actress-producer Lisa Bretz, actor-broadcaster Mike Morris, actor-writer Anthony King, actor-producer Robert Capelli, J. J. Reep, Frank Gorshin and Captain Lou Albano.

Palmer enlarged the agency recently, adding a literary franchise which will possibly benefit her actor clients as well as her screenwriters.

Since Dorothy is seriously committed to the plight of independent filmmakers, she is also always looking for investors.

Agents
Dorothy Palmer
Client List
12 + freelance
Clients
Anthony King, Mike Morris, Robert Capelli, J. J. Reep,
Tony Devon, Nicole Paddington, Holly Farris,
Lisa Bretz, Frank Gorshin and many others

✦ Paradigm

200 W 57th Street, #900
btwn 7th Avenue & Broadway
New York, NY 10019
212-246-1030

Paradigm is the human-size conglomerate that resulted from the amalgamation of four eminent New York and Los Angeles agencies. The wedding involved two elegant talent agencies, Gores/Fields and STE and heavy hitter literary agencies Robinson/Weintraub & Gross and Shorr Stille & Associates).

The original partners of New York's STE, Clifford Stevens and Tex Beha remain in place. Stevens guiding the theatrical department and Beha concentrating on soaps and commercials.

A mainstay of the New York agency scene, the merger only added more power, class and stature to an already top-line agency. New York Paradigm theatrical agents also include Jonathan Bluman, Sarah Fargo (Writers & Artists), Richard Schmenner (STE) and Rosanne Quezada. Schmenner and Quezeda were both franchised at this agency.

Paradigm serves British clients in England as well as those in New York and Los Angeles. Their actors appear to be happy and loyal since Jason Robards and Brian Bedford have been Clifford's clients for over thirty years.

Other names from their prestigious list include Andy Garcia, Campbell Scott, Laurence Fishburne, Eli Wallach, Anne Jackson, Dana Ivey, Max Van Sydow, Jonathon Pryce and Dennis Franz.

Agents
Clifford Stevens, Richard Schmenner, Jonathan Bluman,
Sarah Fargo, Rosanne Quezada and Tex Beha
Client List
60
Clients
Andy Garcia, Jason Robards, Campbell Scott,
Laurence Fishburne, Eli Wallach, Anne Jackson,
Brian Bedford, Dana Ivey, Max Von Sydow,
Jonathon Pryce, Dennis Franz and others

✦ Professional Artists

321 W 44th Street
btwn 8th & 9th Avenues
New York, NY 10036
212-247-8770

Sheldon Lubliner is fun, he's easy to talk to, he's informed, he is a good negotiator and has a good client list. Add charm, taste, ability, access, and a great partner, Marilynn Scott Murphy, and you've pretty much got a picture of Professional Artists. As a director-producer, Sheldon enjoyed all the details involved in mounting shows for Al Pacino, Gene Barry and Vivica Lindfors; he just didn't like raising the money. Deciding he could transfer all his skills into agenting and not be a fundraiser, Sheldon changed careers in 1980 translating his contacts and style into an agency called News and Entertainment. PA is an outgrowth of that venture.

Actress/client, Marilynn Scott Murphy was commandeered to answer phones in a pinch in 1983 and has since become Sheldon's partner. Sheldon's negotiating skills combine with Marilynn's people skills — although they are both strong in this department — *to form the perfect agent*. Their client list includes not only actors, news persons, and radio personalities but also writers, producers and casting directors. Their colleague is Julie Rosner.

Agents
Sheldon Lubliner, Marilynn Scott Murphy and
Julie Rosner
Client List
100
Clients
David Canary, Michael Constantine, Betty Garrett,
Maurice Godin, Mike O'Malley and others

✦ Rachael's Talent Agency, Inc./RTA

134 W 29th Street
btwn 6th & 7th Avenues
New York, NY 10001
212-967-0665

In 1995 Rachel Lis worked at Click representing clients for modeling. As their beauties began having babies, Rachel began finding offers for the tots and soon, with her mother Eunice Butt as partner, they opened their own agency out of their home. They did so well, that six months later, they opened their own space at the present address and hired Jessica Leigh-Weiner (SSC&N) to represent clients for film, theatre and television.

Originally named Rachel's Tots 'N Teens, the agency is still primarily thought of for younger clients, but now also represents children, teens, young adults and adults for commercials, voice-overs, print and some film and television. They have no Equity affiliation.

The list is freelance working primarily through managers. RTA looks at all pictures and resumes and as with other children's agencies says that snapshots are fine to send in search of a meeting.

Agents
Eunice Butt, Rachel Lis and Jessica Leigh-Weiner
Client List
Freelance
Clients
Freelance

✦ Shelly Rothman

101 W 57th Street, 11 E
at 6th Avenue
New York, NY 10019
212-246-2180

Shelly Rothman is one of the few variety agents still operating as an independent instead of a conglomerate. Shelly became an agent by accident. Just out of the Navy in 1944, he landed a job as a gofer for a variety talent agency. Three years later he joined IFA as a variety agent booking comics and singers that worked cabarets, nightclubs, the Catskills, etc.

Shelly works with a select list of comics and singers booking them for personal appearances, but has been known to help struggling performers by pointing them out to people interested in developing new talent.

Agents
Shelly Rothman
Client List
28
Clients
Corbett Monica, Julius LaRosa, Rosemary Clooney, Sal Richards, Bob Melvin and others

✦ Sames & Rollnick Associates

250 W 57th Street, #703
at Broadway
New York, NY 10017
212-315-4434

Mary Sames and Diana Rollnick were colleagues
at Gary Leaverton when they decided to form Sames &
Rollnick Associates in 1985. Since that time, their reputation and client list have grown in stature and credibility.
Colleague Peter Sherwood, began his agenting career here
as an intern.

Sames and Rollnick is a successful, well-thought-
of agency that appears to be accessible, nurturing, and
very connected to the lives of their clients.

Clients from their list include Mike Burstyn,
Henderson Forsyth, Jonathan Freeman, Maureen Moore,
John McMartin, Jamey Sheridan, Heather Robison, Kelli
James Chase, Glen Douglas and Donovan Knowles.

S&R freelances only if they are interested in
eventually signing the client. Los Angeles agencies that
have liaison arrangements with S&R are The Artists
Agency, Gold/Marshak and Schiowitz Clay.

Agents
Mary Sames, Diana Rollnick and Peter Sherwood
Client List
80-95
Clients
Henderson Forsyth, Mike Burstyn, Jonathan Freeman,
Maureen Moore, John McMartin, Jamey Sheridan,
Heather Robison, Kelli James Chase, Glen Douglas,
Donovan Knowles and others

✦ The Sanders Agency, Ltd.

1204 Broadway, #306
btwn 29th & 30th Streets
New York, NY 10001
212-779-3737

Honey Sanders was a working actress in 1978 when her agent (Francie Hidden at Richard Pitman Agency) became ill. Because Honey understood the business and liked people, she volunteered to run the office. She'd already been instrumental in landing jobs for lots of her friends, so why not get paid for it? While Francie was ill, Honey divided her time between agenting and acting. When Francie died, Honey made a career choice and became a full time agent.

Honey runs the Los Angeles office now, leaving daughter, Barbara in charge of things in New York. Leo Simard, who followed in Honey's footsteps as client turned agent, joins Barbara repping Sanders' clients.

The Sanders Agency, Ltd. handles freelance people as well as signed clients.

Agents
Barbara Sanders and Leo Simard
Client List
50 + freelance
Clients
Check Screen Actors Guild listings

✦ William Schill Agency, Inc.

250 W 57th Street, #2402
at Broadway
New York, NY 10019
212-315-5919

After working as a stage manager for 26 years, William Schill decided to take all the resourcefulness he had acquired and perfected while making sure actors got onstage at the right time, saying the right words with the right props and use those skills making sure the actors got the right job at the right money. That was back in 1984 and Schill hasn't looked back.

He feels his years of stage managing affect his actor-perspective, giving him *an edge in spotting talent.* Though he continues to work extensively with freelance talent, Schill has 35 signed clients that he represents for theatre, film and television. His interesting contributions elsewhere in the book regarding things actors can do to help themselves are right on the money. Be sure to check them out.

Agents
William Schill
Client List
35 + freelance
Clients
Jeremy Zeliq, Larry Small, Carleton Carpenter, Mercedes Perez, Jeremiah Johnston and others

✦ Silver Massetti Szatmary & Associates/East Ltd.

145 W 45th Street, #1204
btwn 6th & 7th Avenues
New York, NY 10030
212-391-4545

Monty Silver expected that his background as an actor, stage manager, graduate school scenic designer and gofer on Broadway would lead to a career in producing. It has. His distinguished agency has not only produced some important actors, but some prestigious agents as well.

Figuring to round out his show-biz education with a six-month stint at agenting, he accepted Hilly Elkins' offer in 1957 and has been at it ever since, starting his own agency in 1961.

Monty's Los Angeles office is run by former subagent/now-partner Donna Massetti. Silver's New York clients are repped by Monty as well as ex-casting director, Dianne Busch, ex-actor Michael Kelly Boone (who was in the antique business before becoming an assistant at this agency) and Meg Bucknam, who was an assistant at Lionel Larner.

One of the most successful and respected agents in the business, Silver represents an illustrious list and freelances with a few other actors whose careers he believes in. His favorite client is one who continues to perfect his craft. Silver feels this kind of client is always in the mainstream because of constant study.

Agents
Monty Silver, Michael Kelly Boone, Dianne Busch and
Meg Bucknam
Client List
85
Clients
David Hyde-Pierce, Paul Guilfoyle, James Rebhorn,
Zeljko Ivanek, Celeste Holm, Fyvush Finkel,
Laura Linney and others

✦ The Tantleff Office

375 Greenwich Street, #700
S of 14th Street/W of Hudson
New York, NY 10013
212-941-3939

Located in the same building as the trendy Tribeca Grill, just visiting The Tantleff Office is enough to make you feel that you will be a star immediately. With the connections and clients this agency has, if you are talented, that might not be far off the mark.

Before opening his own literary agency in 1986, Jack Tantleff worked as a general manager, a company manager and as an assistant at two legendary agencies: Hesseltine Baker and STE .

The theatrical department at this agency which opened in 1994 is beginning to gather momentum led by former personal manager, Robyne Kintz (DGRW) and Bill Timms (Sames & Rolnick, Writers & Artists).

Since the agency has literary clients like Marsha Norman (*'night, Mother, The Secret Garden*), Brian Friel (*Dancing at Lughnasa*), Arthur Kopit (*Phantom, Nine, Wings*), Henry Krieger (*Dreamgirls*) and Lucy Simon (*The Secret Garden*), Bill and Robyne have an inside track on material in development and early access to casting.

Technologically au courante, Bill and Robyne have managed to become connected to the Los Angeles casting community via The Internet and have the bookings to prove it.

Clients at this agency include Rachel York, Alma Cuervo, Pamela Isaacs (Tony-nominated actress for *The Life*) and Ross Lehman (*A Funny Thing Happened on the Way to the Forum*).

This office represents actors, directors, authors, scriptwriters and composers/songwriters. They see new clients mainly by referral, but do look at pictures and resumes carefully.

Agents
Robyne Kintz and Bill Timms
Client List
50
Clients
Rachel York, Alma Cuervo, Pamela Isaacs, Ross Lehman
and others

✦ Talent Representatives, Inc.

20 E 53rd Street
just E of 5th Avenue
New York, NY 10022
212-752-1835

Honey Raider is the sole owner of this thriving agency since partner Steve Kaplan died in 1993. They had been together since 1964 when the two were briefly selling real estate. Their mutual love of theatre, film, and television led them to choose agenting as a way to become involved in show business.

Glen Barnard was a production assistant at Lancit Media Productions before joining TRI as an assistant in December of 1990. Jerre Brisky was an associate business manager prior to joining with Honey and Glen to rep such clients as Donald May, Kale Browne, Walt Willey, David Forsyth, Judi Evans, Colleen Dion, Lauren Martin-Harkins and others.

Talent Representatives also handle writers, directors and producers.

Agents
Honey Raider, Glen Barnard and Jerre Brisky
Client List
17 + freelance
Clients
Donald May, Kale Browne, Walt Willey, David Forsyth, Judi Evans, Colleen Dion, Lauren Martin-Harkins and others

✦ Michael Thomas Agency, Inc.

305 Madison Avenue, #4419
at 42nd Street
New York, NY 10165-4419
212-867-0303

Michael Thomas came to New York from
Georgia to pursue a career onstage. After a brief stint
acting, he began his agenting career with Fifi Oscard
Associates in 1960. Six years later, he opened MTA, Inc.

Michael has assisted the careers of countless
important actors, not the least of whom is Lynne
Thigpen who thanked Michael on national television
when she won the 1997 Tony for best featured actress in
An American Daughter.

In addition to Lynn, Michael's clients include
Edward Norton (NY only) and John McDonough
(*Captain Kangaroo*).

Rozanne Gates has been Michael's colleague for
twelve years. Annette Shear assists both agents. Michael
works with signed clients as well as freelance. He and
Rozanne check all pictures and resumes carefully.

Agents
Michael Thomas and Rozanne Gates
Client List
20 + freelance
Clients
Lynne Thigpen, Edward Norton (NY only),
John McDonough and others

◆ Trawick Artists Management, Inc.

1926 Broadway, 6th floor
across from Lincoln Center at 65th St.
New York, NY 10023
212-874-2482

Brenda Trawick opened Trawick Artists Management in 1983 to represent classical musicians and opera
singers. When the hit show, *The Master Class* required
actors with classical voices, casting directors naturally
turned to Brenda.

After placing client Jay Hunter Morris in *Master
Class* Brenda decided that she wanted to represent actors
as well as opera singers, so she hired Gloria Bonelli
(Peggy Hadley) in April of 1996 to develop a theatrical
department for her agency.

Gloria's colleague, Gina Makowski worked in
commercials at J. Michael Bloom and in legit at William
Morris before casting at NW Ayer Advertising.

Gloria and Gina shepherd a list of about 20
signed clients. Since they are a new agency, they are still
shaping their roster of actors and expect the ultimate list
to be about 50. While they are building their list, they are
working with some actors on a freelance basis to
determine their suitability as signed clients. Their clients
work chiefly in television and theatre and do quite well in
the independent film market in New York. Gloria and
Gina have set up relationships with liaison agents in Los
Angeles so that their clients will have the benefit of bi-
coastal representation.

Gloria and Gina pride themselves on their hands-
on managerial relationship with their clients. Clients from
their list include Carlos Leon (*Big Levowski*), Jason
Robards III (*Dark Tides*), Manny Perez (*Courage Under
Fire*), Karenjune (*Sanchez*), Brenda Burke (*Carmen
SanDiego*) Kim O'Mara (*Frogs & Snakes*) and stand-up

Bernadette Pauley.

Pictures that appeal to this office are those taken in natural light that are more than head shots. Gloria likes ¾ body perhaps with something a little different about them. Gloria and Gina are assisted by recent NYU Arts Administration graduate, Deb Malkin.

TAM, Inc. is opening a Los Angeles office soon.

Agents
Gloria Bonelli and Gina Makowski
Client List
going to 50
Clients
Jason Robards III, Carlos Leon, Karenjune, Manny Perez, Brenda Burke, Kim O'Mara, Bernadette Pauley and others

✦ Waters and Nicolosi

1501 Broadway, #1305
btwn 43rd & 44th Streets
New York, NY 10036
212-302-8787

Actor/employment representative, Bob Waters is a man with an understanding wife. When Bob saw an ad for a job in *The New York Times* for a theatrical trainee and it was strictly commission, Waters' wife (and the mother of his four children) encouraged him to go for it. She figured this was a way to combine his day job and showbusiness. The rest, as they say, is history.

Waters opened The Waters Agency in 1969. The name of the business changed in 1993 reflecting the longtime collaboration with colleague Jeanne Nicolosi.

Shawna McCormack (Funny Face) heads the Soap Department while John Woodward (who was a manager with Nanni Saperstein Management) guides the Young Performer department.

W&N boasts a list of about 60-65 happy signed clients. Waters says his clients seem to *stay a long time and enjoy the association.* This agency no longer handles freelancers.

Clients of Waters & Nicolosi include Jennifer Garner (*Significant Others*), Shiek Mahmud-Bey (*The Profiler*), Maureen Stapleton, Justin Chambers (*Another World*), and four-time Obie winner, Jeff Weiss.

A man who knows how to get what he wants, Waters is charming and persistent. I think what I like best about him is that with all the things he has going for him, he still considers his greatest asset to be his wife.

Agents
Bob Waters, Jeanne Nicolosi, Shawna McCormack and
John Woodward
Client List
60-65
Clients
Maureen Stapleton, Jennifer Garner, Shiek Mahmud-Bey,
Justin Chambers, Jeff Weiss and others

◆ WMA/William Morris Agency

1350 Avenue of the Americas
at 54th Street
New York, NY 10019
212-586-5100

There really was a man named William Morris who started this agency in 1898. During the 100 years since, although WMA has had it's ups and downs, down was never further than #3. Today, WMA, ICM and CAA are probably more equal in power and prestige than they have been in 20 years.

In late 1992, in an effort to regroup what many were describing as a has-been agency, WMA merged with the prestigious boutique agency, Triad in a bid to capture more big names. The Los Angeles Times states that *overall revenues at the agency have increased 65% since the Triad acquisition.*

Along with star clients who joined the agency at that point, WMA captured brilliant new agents, not the least of which was Triad partner and now head of the motion picture division and president of William Morris, Arnold Rifkin.

Credited with engineering the renewed visibility and power of John Travolta and Sylvester Stallone, Rifkin created an independent film department. He and his staff helped put together such films as *Pulp Fiction, The English Patient* and *Sling Blade.*

Other top dogs at WMA are Norman Browkow, chairman of the agency, Jerry Katzman, who packaged *The Cosby Show* and *Roseanne,* and Walter Zifkin, who played a big role in the acquisition of Triad.

The agency represents not only actors, writers, directors and producers, but athletes, newscasters, political figures and almost any other being of notoriety.

If having the most agents means you have the

most power, WMA wins hands down. On a list of agents I looked at, WMA had 222 as compared to 94 at ICM and 113 at CAA. Of course, CAA only has the Los Angeles office, while WMA has offices on both coasts. In any event, the number of agents is pretty staggering. I'm not going to attempt to list all the names. Not only is the list confidential, it's way too long. If you want a detailed up to the minute list, get my favorite resource book for this information, *Hollywood Agents & Managers Directory* published by The Hollywood Creative Directory. The HCD somehow manage to penetrate the iron curtain. Their book tracks the names of conglomerate agents very effectively.

Agents
Todd Harris, Jeff Hunter, Nicole David,
Gene Parseghian, John Kimble, Arnold Rifkin,
David Kalodner, Marcy Posner, Perri Kipperman,
Michael August, Beth Blickers, Bill Contardi,
James Dixon, Mary Meagher, Johnnie Planco,
Jane Rosenberg and many, many more
Client List
More and more every day
Clients
Daniel Day-Lewis, Christopher Walken, Peter Barnes,
Henry Bromwell, Emma Thompson, Matthew Modine,
Lili Taylor, Ashley Judd, Arnold Schwarzenegger,
Cary Brokaw, Robert Altman, John Rubinstein,
Daphne Maxwell Reid, John Travolta, Bruce Willis,
Julianne Moore, Tim Burton, Clint Eastwood,
Stephen Frears, Diane Keaton, John Malkovich,
Walter Matthau, Tim Reid, Alec Baldwin, Willem Dafoe,
Danny Aiello, Charlie Sheen, Dean Stockwell,
Candice Bergen and many others

✦ Ann Wright Representatives

165 W 46th Street, #1105
just E of Broadway, in the Equity Building
New York, NY 10036
212-764-6770

When Ann Wright came to New York after training as an actress at prestigious Boston University, she joined the casting pool for CBS. Like many other actors who have an opportunity to explore other areas of the business, she decided there were other ways to use her creative skills. She assisted legendary agent, Milton Goldman and cast commercials at an advertising agency before she became a commercial agent. She also worked for both Charles Tranum and Bret Adams before opening her own agency.

This agency is specifically thought of for voice-over and commercial talent, however, the legit department started by Susan Barry-Mayo, continues to flourish in the hands of her successor, Fritz Collester (Hodges Talent).

The growing theatrical list at this agency includes Renee Joshua Porter, Etain O'Malley, George Artenleff, Yuval Zamir, Mary Shultz, Peggy Gormley, Billie Allen and Herab Rubena.

Fritz works with both signed and freelance clients and looks carefully at all pictures and resumes.

Agents
Fritz Collester
Client List
15 + freelance
Clients
Renee Joshua Porter, Etain O'Malley, George Artenleff, Yuval Zamir, Mary Shultz, Peggy Gormley, Billie Allen and Herab Rubena.

✦ Writers & Artists Agency

19 W 44th Street, #1000
just W of 5th Avenue
New York, NY 10036
212-391-1112

Originally known as The Joan Scott Agency when dynamo Joan Scott created this office in the 1960s, the name was soon changed to reflect the addition of distinguished writers and directors to Scott's client list.

Champions of New York's busy independent film business, Writers & Artists has been cited by both *Daily Variety* and *The Hollywood Reporter* as being at the center of Manhattan's independent film scene.

W&A's list sports actors Mary Alice, Estelle Parsons, Joe Mantello, Elina Lowensohn, Vincent Laresca, John Cullum, Brendan Sexton, Hope Davis, Lauren Graham, Elizabeth Ashley as well as *SNL* performers like Cheri Oteri and Siobhan Fallon, so it's easy to see W&A is eclectic in their approach.

This office is also home to directors Jerry Zaks and Walter Bobbie.

There are five theatrical agents in the New York office to shepherd the 50-60 New York based members of the W&A client list: Jason Goudgeon was in the Los Angeles office before joining Linda Jacobs Kalodner (Sames & Rollnick, Peter Strain) Rob Pattillo (who was in development at Miramax/Dimensions), Jeffrey Berger (ICM) and Robert Meder who was franchised at this agency.

Writers & Artists works with signed clients only.

Agents

Linda Jacobs Kalodner, Jason Goudgeon, Rob Pattillo,
Robert Meder and Jeffrey Berger

Client List

150 (both coasts)

Clients

Danton Stone, Elina Lowensohn, Vincent Laresca,
Estelle Parsons, John Cullum, Brendon Sexton, Cheri
Oteri, Joe Mantello, Hope Davis, Lauren Graham,
Siobhan Fallon, Elizabeth Ashley, Mary Alice and others

✦ Zoli Management, Inc.

3 W 18th Street, 5th Floor
just W of 5th Avenue
New York, NY 10011-4610
212-242-1500

This famous modeling agency continues to
represent the young and beautiful for theatre, film,
television and commercials. The agency was founded in
1970 by Zoli Redessy, but former employees Barbara
Lantz and Victoria Pribble became the owners when Zoli
died in 1980 and left the business to them. When Victoria
died, Barbara became the sole owner.

Today the agency is run by Roseanne Vecchione,
who heads the men's division and Rosemarie Chalem
who directs the women's department. Although this
agency previously handled print only, Vecchione and
Chalem have now turned their sights to theatre, film,
television and commercials.

Vecchione says she would love to represent
character people, she says that since Zoli's reputation is
for beautiful people, it's rare when she gets a phone call
for anything else.

If you're Y&B, however, Zoli could be a good
idea. They only work with freelance talent.

With the addition of agents, Paul Blasick,
Darren Jenkins, Joanne Kalwoncu and Henry Ravello, it's
clear that the film and television thrust is humming.

Agents
Roseanne Vecchione, Rosemarie Chalem, Paul Blasick,
Darren Jenkins, Joanne Kalwoncu and Henry Ravello
Client List
Freelance
Clients
Young and beautiful

✦ Glossary

Academy Players Directory — Catalogue of actors published annually for the Los Angeles market. Shows one or two pictures per actor and lists credits and representation. If you work freelance, you can list your name and service. Some list union affiliation. Casting directors, producers and whomever else routinely keeps track of actors use the book as a reference guide. Every actor who is ready to book should either be in this directory or the New York counterpart is The Players Guide.

Actors' Unions —There are three: *Actors Equity Association* (commonly referred to as Equity) is the union that covers actors' employment in the theatre. *American Federation of Television and Radio Artists* (commonly referred to as AFTRA) covers actors employed in videotape and radio. *Screen Actors Guild* (commonly referred to as SAG) covers actors employed in theatrical motion pictures and all filmed television product.

Audition Tape — Also known as a Composite Cassette Tape. A videotape usually no longer than six minutes, showcasing either one performance or a montage of scenes of an actor's work. Agents and casting directors prefer tapes of professional appearances (film or television), but some will look at a tape produced for audition purposes only. Usually on VHS.

Breakdown Service — Started in 1971 by Gary Marsh, the Service condenses scripts and lists parts available in films, television and theatre. Expensive and available to agents and managers only.

Clear — The unions require that the agent check with a freelance actor (clearing) before submitting him on a particular project.

Composite Cassette Tape — See Audition Tape.

Equity-Waiver Productions — See Showcases.

Freelance — Term used to describe the relationship between an actor and agent or agents who submit the actor for work without an exclusive contract. New York agents frequently will work on this basis, Los Angeles agents rarely consent to this arrangement.

Going Out — Auditions or meetings with directors and/or casting directors. These are usually set up by your agent but have also been set up by very persistent and courageous actors.

The Leagues — A now defunct formal collective of prestigious theatre schools that offer conservatory training for the actor. The schools still exist, but there is no longer an association. As far as agents are concerned, this is the very best background an actor can have, other than having your father own a studio. Schools in this collective are American Conservatory Theatre in San Francisco, CA; American Repertory Theatre, Harvard University in Cambridge, MA; Boston University in Boston, MA; Carnegie-Mellon in Pittsburgh, PA; Catholic University in Washington, DC; The Juilliard School in New York City, NY; New York University in New York City, NY; North Carolina School of the Arts in Winston-Salem, NC; Southern Methodist University in Dallas, TX; The University of California at San Diego in La Jolla, CA and the Yale Drama School in New Haven, CT. Addresses are listed in Chapter Seven.

Letter of Termination — A legal document dissolving the contract between actor and agent. If you decide to leave your agent while your current contract is in effect, it is usually possible to do so citing Paragraph 6 of the SAG Agency Regulations. Paragraph 6 allows either the actor or the agent to terminate the contract if the actor has not worked for more than 15 of the previous 91 days by sending a letter of termination. Your letter should say something like:

Dear :

This is to inform you that relative to Paragraph 6 of the Screen Actors Basic Contract, I am terminating our contract as of this date.

Send a copy of the letter to your agent via registered mail, return receipt requested, plus a copy to the Screen Actors Guild and all other unions involved. Retain a copy for your files.

Major Role/Top of the Show — A predetermined fee set by producers which, in most cases, is a non-negotiable maximum for guest appearances on television episodes. See minimums.

Membership Requirements for Actors' Equity — Rules for membership state you must have a verifiable Equity Contract in order to join or have been a member in good standing for at least one year in AFTRA or SAG.
Initiation fee is currently $800, payable prior to election to membership. Basic dues are $37 twice a year. Additionally, there are working dues: 2% of gross weekly earnings from employment is deducted from your check just like your income tax.

Membership Requirements for AFTRA — are pretty lenient and seem to be based on having the money to pay the enrollment fee. (Note: It can be a hindrance to join unions before you are ready as that puts you out of the running to do non-union films, shows, etc., and amass film on yourself.) Check with the AFTRA office for specifics on membership requirements. AFTRA's initiation fee is $800. Dues are payable semi-annually and are based on the performer's gross earnings under AFTRA's jurisdiction for the previous year. The lowest amount of annual dues (on earnings up to $2,000) is $84. If you make over $100,000, you pay $1,000.

Membership Requirements for Screen Actors Guild — The most prized union card is Screen Actors Guild. Actors may join upon proof of employment or prospective employment within two weeks or less of start date of a SAG signatory film, television program or commercial.

Proof of employment may be in the form of a signed contract, a payroll check or check stub, or a letter from the company (on company letterhead stationery). The document proving employment must state the applicant's name, Social Security number, the name of the production or commercial, the salary paid in dollar amount and the dates worked.

Another way of joining SAG is by being a paid up member of an affiliated performers' union for a period of at least one year, having worked at least once as a principal performer in that union's jurisdiction.

1.   Screen Actors Guild Initiation Fee as of 7-1-97 is $1,160.50. This seems like a lot of money (and is) but the formula involved makes some sense. It is SAG minimum ($559 for two days work ($1,118) plus the first semiannual dues ($42.50). This money is payable in full, in cashier's check or money order, at the time of application. The fees may be lower in some branch areas. SAG dues are based on SAG earnings and are billed twice a year. Those members earning more than $5,000 annually under SAG contracts will pay 1½% of all money earned in excess of $5,000 up to a maximum of $150,000. If you are not working, you can go on *Honorary Withdrawal* which *only*

relieves you of the obligation to pay your dues. You are still in the union and prohibited from accepting non-union work.

Equity Minimum — There are 18 basic contracts ranging from the low end of the Small Production Contract (from $100 to $390 weekly depending on the size of the theatre) to the higher Production Contract covering Broadway houses, Jones Beach, tours, etc. ($1,000 weekly). Highest is the Business Theatre Agreement, for shows produced by large corporations.

AFTRA Minimum — The minimum contract as of 7-1-97 is $559 a day for a commercial. For taped syndicated shows other than commercials, the fee is $485 for ten half-hours over a two-day period. That means they can call you at any time over a 48-hour period and have you work 2 hours and then come back in 4 hours and work for 30 minutes until the job is finished or the ten half-hours are used up. Then they go into overtime. The half-hours do not have to be consecutive. Since AFTRA's pay scale is so complicated (and low), management often plays one union off against the other.

AFTRA Nighttime Rates — for primetime are on a parity with Screen Actors Guild (see their rates). Day rates for soap operas are $402 for a principal role on a half-hour show (based on a 9-hour workday) and $536 for a one-hour show. There are special categories and different fees for announcers, newscasters, singers, chorus, etc., as well as radio and voice over. The fees I am quoting are for straight on-camera acting.

Screen Actors Guild Minimum — As of 7-1-97, SAG Scale rates require $559 daily and $1,942 weekly as a minimum for employment in films and television. Overtime in SAG is considerably higher than in AFTRA.

Open Calls — refer to auditions or meetings held by casting directors that are not restricted by agents. No individual appointments are given. Usually the call is made in an advertisement in one of the trade newspapers, by flyers or in a news story in the popular press. As you can imagine, the number of people that show up is enormous. You will have to wait a long time. Although management's eyes tend to glaze over and see nothing after a certain number of hours, actors do sometimes get jobs this way.

Overexposed — Term used by nervous buyers (producers, casting directors, networks, etc.) indicating an actor has become too recognizable for their tastes. Frequently he just got off another show and everyone remembers him as a particular character and the buyer doesn't want the public thinking of that instead of his project. A thin line exists between not being recognizable and being overexposed.

Packaging — This practice involves a talent agency approaching a buyer with material (writer), a star, usually a star director and possibly a producer already attached to it. May include any number of other writers, actors, producers, etc.

Paid Auditions — There's no formal name for the practice of rounding up 20 actors and charging them $10 each for the privilege of meeting a casting director, agent, producer, etc. There are agents, casting directors and actors who feel the practice is unethical. It does give some actors who would otherwise not be seen an opportunity to meet and be seen by casting directors. I feel meeting a casting director under these circumstances is questionable and that there are more productive ways to spend your money.

Per Diem — Negotiated amount of money for

glossy (or matte) print black and white photograph.

Pilot — The first episode of a proposed television series. Produced so that the network can determine whether there will be additional episodes. There are many pilots made every year. Few go to series. Fewer stay on the air for more than a single season.

Players Guide — Catalogue of actors published annually for the New York market. Shows one or two pictures per actor and lists credits and representation. If you work freelance, you can list your name and service. Some list union affiliation. Casting directors, producers and whomever else routinely keeps track of actors use the book as a reference guide. Every actor who is ready to book, should be in this directory.

Principal — Job designation indicating a part larger than an extra or an *Under Five.*

Ready to Book — Agent talk for an actor who has been trained and judged mature enough to handle himself well in the audition, not only with material, but also with the buyers. Frequently refers to an actor whose progress in acting class or theatre has been monitored by the agent.

Resume — The actor's ID, lists credits, physical description, agent's name and phone contact.

Right — When someone describes an actor as being *right* for a part, he is speaking about the essence of an actor. We all associate a particular essence with Brad Pitt and a different essence with Jim Carrey. One would not expect Pitt and Carrey to be up for the same part. Being *right* also involves credits. The more important the part, the more credits are necessary to support being seen.

Being *right* also involves credits. The more important the part, the more credits are necessary to support being seen.

Rollcall — is like *The Players Guide* and *The Academy Players Directory* except pictures and information are fed into subscribers' computers. The advantage is you can update your resume as often as you like. Lots of differing opinions on this. Some agents think it's stupid. I don't see the harm. It doesn't cost that much to be listed and many important buyers subscribe.

Scale — See minimums.

Showcases — Productions in which members of Actors Equity are allowed by the union to work without compensation are called Showcases in New York and 99-Seat Theatre Plan in Los Angeles. Equity members are allowed to perform as long as the productions conform to certain Equity guidelines: rehearsal conditions, limiting the number of performances and seats and providing a set number of complimentary tickets for industry people. The producers must provide tickets for franchised agents, casting directors and producers. There is a maximum ticket price of $12.

Sides — The pages of script containing your audition material. Usually not enough information to use as a source to do a good audition. If they won't give you a complete script, go early (or the day before), sit in the office and read it. SAG rules require producers to allow actors access to the script (if it's written).

Stage Time — Term used to designate the amount of time a performer has had in front of an audience. Most agents and casting executives believe that an actor can only achieve a certain level of confidence by amassing stage time. They're right.

Submissions — Sending an actor's name to a casting director in hopes of getting the actor an audition or meeting for a part.

Talent — Management's synonym for actors.

Top of the Show/Major Role — A predetermined fee set by producers which is a non-negotiable maximum for guest appearances on television episodes. Also called Major Role Designation.

The Trades — *Backstage* and *ShowBusiness* are newspapers that cover all kinds of show business news. Los Angeles counterparts are *Dramalogue* and *Backstage West*. They list information about classes, auditions, casting, etc. These publications are particularly helpful to newcomers. All are available at good newsstands or by subscription.

Under Five — An AFTRA job in which the actor has five or fewer lines. Paid at a specific rate — less than a principal and more than an extra. Sometimes referred to as Five and Under.

Visible/Visibility — Currently on view in film, theatre or television. In this business, it's *out of sight, out of mind*, so visibility is very important.

99-Seat Theatre Plan — The Los Angeles version of the *Showcase*. Originally called waiver. Producers give actors an expense reimbursement of $5-$14 per performance. It's not much, but it adds up; at least you're not working for free.

Producers must also conform to Equity guidelines regarding rehearsal conditions, number of performances, complimentary tickets for industry, etc. If you participate in this plan, be sure to stop by Equity and get a copy of your rights.

✦ Index to Agents/Agencies

Barnard, Glen, 250
Barry Agency, 169
Barry Haft Brown, 155, 169, 210
Barry, Bob, 155, 169
Barry-Mayo, Susan, 258
Basch, Richard, 179
Baum, Martin, 226
Bauman Hiller & Associates, 167
Bauman, Dick, 167
Beha, Tex, 238, 239
Beilin, Peter, 63, 77, 81, 170
Berg, Phil, 222
Berg-Allenberg Agency, 222
Berger, Jeffrey, 259, 260
Berman, Boals and Flynn, Inc., 20, 50, 52, 95, 173
Berman, Lois, 173
Bertalovitz, Gary, 228
Bethel Agencies, 171
Big Duke 6 Artists Inc., 175
Black, Claudia, 207
Blasick, Paul, 261
Blickers, Beth, 257
Bloom, J. Michael, 49, 177, 201
Bluman, Jonathan, 238, 239
Boals, Judy, 173
Boatwright, Boaty, 209
Bonelli, Gloria, 253
Boone, Michael Kelly, 246, 247
Bordalo, Ann, 230
Brisky, Jerre, 250, 251
Bronfin, Arthur, 228
Browkow, Norman, 256
Brown, Justin, 193
Brown, Nanci, 155, 169
Bruce Levy Agency, 227
Buchwald, Don, 179, 189
Bucknam, Meg, 246
Burton-Carson, Maria, 184, 185

✦ Index to Agents for Stand-Ups

✦ Index to Agents for Children

✦ Index to Everything Else